DIVINE KARMA

The Dream of Life

DAVID RAMIREZ

The Dream of Life

Book Three of the Divine Karma Trilogy

ISBN: 978-0-9983932-8-5

Divine Karma
13611 South Dixie Hwy. Suite 453
Miami, Florida 33176 USA
www.Divine-Karma.com

The Divine Karma Trilogy:
Book One: Divine Karma: The Journey of Self-Discovery
Book Two: The Journey Towards Enlightenment
Book Three: The Dream of Life

DEDICATION

To my beloved wife, Patrycja: you sacrificed everything because you believed in me. In your love I found the courage to write these words, and in your unwavering faith I found the strength to finish them. This book is as much yours as it is mine. You are my home.

To my children (Achilles, Noah, and Livia), you are my greatest teachers and my deepest inspiration. Watching you grow has shown me more about awakening than any philosophy ever could. You are living proof that love creates worlds.

You are my universe. You are my inspiration.

Table of Contents

Introduction

Dear Reader,

You didn't pick up this book by accident. Something, maybe a whisper, maybe a storm, brought you here. And if you're holding these pages now, it means you're ready to remember. What if the life you think you are living is only a fragment of a much larger, unseen truth? What if everything you were taught to believe, about the world, about yourself, about reality, was merely a veil covering something far more expansive, more divine, and more extraordinary?

The Dream of Life is not a book of answers; it is an invitation to question. It is a journey through the illusions that shape our identity, the matrix that defines our society, and the spiritual truths hidden beneath the noise of modern life. Drawing from science, metaphysics, philosophy, and ancient teachings, this book seeks to guide you back to what has always been within you: awareness, sovereignty, and divine intelligence.

Each chapter peels back a layer of the dream, revealing how deeply consciousness is entangled in the experience of being human. You'll explore the architecture of belief, the mechanics of manifestation, the mystery of quantum reality, and the soul's eternal journey through time, space, and memory. This book was written not to teach you something new, but to help you remember something ancient, that you are the dreamer, not the dream. You are the creator, not the creation. You are not here to escape this world, but to awaken within it.

If you have walked with me through *Divine Karma: The Journey of Self-Discovery* and *The Journey Towards Enlightenment*, you already know the road that brought us here. In the first book, we uncovered the karmic blueprint woven into every human experience and discovered that the divine you had been searching for was never outside of you. In the second, we entered the grand game of consciousness, the simulation of existence, and arrived at a truth left deliberately unfinished: *"The simulation ends the moment you remember: you are the creator, not just the player."* This book is what you remember. This is the third movement: not merely discovering the divine within, not only recognizing the game, but learning to live, breathe, and create as the awakened dreamer. If this is where your journey with these ideas begins, everything you need is within these pages. And if you are returning, welcome home.

Welcome to the journey of remembrance. The truth has always been waiting for you, beneath the noise, beyond the veil, and inside the dream.

In sacred remembrance, David Ramirez

Chapter 1: The Dream of Matter

"What we call reality is an agreement of perception."

Awakening Through Perception

We begin this journey with a paradox: the world you see, the body you inhabit, the ground beneath your feet, none of it is what it seems. What appears solid is mostly space. What feels fixed is actually flowing. What we call matter is a dream condensed into form. This isn't poetry. It's physics. Quantum mechanics, the most successful theory in modern science, tells us that the material world is not built from tiny particles but from fields of probability. That matter doesn't exist in a definite state until it is observed. That the act of observation itself collapses potential into reality.

To awaken is to recognize this not only intellectually, but experientially. To begin to feel, sense, and live as if what we once believed was external and fixed is internal and fluid. The world is not happening to us. It is arising within us. We are not living in reality. We are participating in its construction.

—

The Illusion of Solidity

We were taught that the world is made of stuff, atoms, molecules, matter. But when we look closer, even the densest object is mostly empty space. The atom is 99.9999999% void. What we perceive as solid is simply energy vibrating at a frequency slow enough to appear tangible. So, what gives form its structure? Our perception. Our expectations. Our conditioning. This is what the mystics and sages have always known: that the world is a projection. A mirror. A reflection of mind, emotion, and spirit.

The Buddha called this world *maya*, illusion. Jesus referred to it as the world of Caesar, separate from the kingdom within. Hindu scriptures describe it as *Lila*, the divine play. All point to the same truth: what we think is real is only temporarily, experientially so. It is a construct, a dream we forgot we were dreaming. And yet, this dream is not meaningless. It is not random. It is alive with purpose and guided by intelligence. It is your mirror, your teacher, your testing ground. It shows you exactly where your consciousness is resonating, and offers you the opportunity to evolve it.

—

Matter as Frozen Light

Science now confirms what ancient texts hinted at: matter is energy. And energy is light. Everything that exists arises from the quantum field, a sea of vibrating potential. When consciousness interacts with this field, waves become particles. Light becomes mass. Form is born. We could say: matter is frozen light. And just as ice melts into water and then evaporates into vapor, so too can form dissolve into energy, and energy into pure potential.

You are not a thing. You are a process. A movement. A field of conscious awareness sculpting energy into shape. You were never meant to fit into the mold of matter. You were meant to awaken to your role in shaping it. The more you awaken, the less attached you become to things, possessions, roles, even your own body. Not because they don't matter, but because you realize you are the one giving them meaning.

—

The Observer Effect

In the famous double-slit experiment, electrons are fired through two slits, creating a wave-like interference pattern. But when observed, when measured, they collapse into particle behavior. The mere act of observation changes the outcome. This isn't metaphor. It's been tested, repeated, and confirmed. What does this mean? That reality is not independent of your awareness. That the universe is responsive. That what you expect to see, you reinforce into being.

The observer is not passive. The observer is creative. You are not watching the movie. You are writing the script. This realization brings enormous responsibility. If your consciousness influences what becomes "real," then your beliefs, your emotions, and your attention are not trivial, they are tools of creation. The world bends to your vibration, not because it is yours alone, but because it is shared. You are entangled with everything you see. You are part of the equation. The more conscious you become of your role, the more powerfully you shape the equation's outcome.

—

The Programming of Perception

From birth, we're taught how to see. What to call things. What is valuable. What is dangerous. These mental models become filters, shaping our experience. We believe in separation because we were taught it. We believe in limitations because they were modeled. We believe in death because it is all we've seen. But belief is not truth. It is agreement. And agreements can be rewritten.

Our perceptions are programmed by repetition, trauma, and culture. Most people live in a trance, reacting to patterns and signals they've never consciously examined. To awaken is to begin asking: "Where did I learn to see this way?" We don't see the world as it is. We see the world as we are. And if we are fragmented, afraid, or asleep, so too will our world reflect that.

—

Matter Is Meaning

One of the most important realizations is that the universe is not made of things, it is made of meanings. Every object you encounter is more than its material form. It carries a symbolic signature. A vibration. A lesson. A tree is not just cellulose and bark. It is stillness. Patience. The passage of time. A mirror is not just glass, it is the truth unfiltered. A closed door is not just wood. It is a question.

When you stop seeing matter as meaningless and start seeing it as symbolic, the world comes alive. You are no longer a bystander. You are a participant in an unfolding dialogue. Even illness, pain, and breakdowns are messengers, not punishments. They carry information. They show you where you are out of alignment with truth. When you listen to them, not fight, fear, or fix them, they begin to teach.

—

You Are the Dreamer

Let this land gently: You are not inside a dream. The dream is inside of you. You are not trapped in a simulation. You are simulating reality through your perception. Your body is a bio-receiver, interpreting frequencies. Your mind is a translator, applying meaning. Your emotions are the ink, coloring the experience. You are not a character. You are the author. You are not the effect. You are the cause.

This doesn't mean you control everything. But it does mean that you are co-creating everything. When you look around and see chaos, pause before you react. Ask: "What part of me is this reflecting?" Not as blame, but as inquiry. What are you being invited to heal, to feel, or to release? The world is your canvas. Your breath is the brush. Your belief is the color.

—

Practical Awakening: Working with the Dream

So, what do you do with this knowledge? You begin to live more consciously. You question your assumptions. You observe your emotions. You shift your language from victimhood to authorship. You stop saying "this is just how it is," and start asking, "what else is possible?" You begin to declutter your attention. You begin to slow down. You stop treating your body like a machine and start treating it like an altar.

You watch what you consume, not only with your mouth, but with your mind. You choose your thoughts the way you'd choose ingredients for a sacred meal. You become aware of your field, your emotional signature, and you take responsibility for cleaning it. You do not do this to become perfect. You do this to become present. And presence is what collapses the illusion.

—

Reflection: The Dreamer Stirs

- Matter is not solid, it is potential. Perception shapes experience. Observation collapses possibility into form. You are not the result of the dream. You are its source. The more aware you become, the more fluid reality becomes. You are the sculptor of your own simulation. You are the one who remembers the illusion, and remembers your power. This is not theory. This is training. You are learning how to become lucid within the illusion. Not to escape it, but to play more masterfully within it.

Welcome to the first ripple of remembrance. The dream is waking. And so are you. You have been on this journey longer than you may realize, and this is where it arrives.

Chapter 2: The Illusion of Control

"Control is not the path to freedom. Surrender is."

We live in a world that teaches us early: if you want to be safe, you must control. Control your emotions. Control your outcomes. Control your image, your finances, your relationships, your body, your time. Entire industries are built on the promise that if you just control enough variables, you can finally relax. But true peace never comes that way. Because control is a mask for fear. It is the ego's attempt to prevent the unknown. It is the illusion that if we tighten our grip, we will be spared from pain. But the paradox is this: the tighter we grip; the more life resists us. What we try to control begins to control us.

Awakening begins the moment we realize this. When we begin to see that life is not something we must dominate, but something we must dance with.

—

The Programming of Control

From childhood, we are rewarded for compliance and punished for spontaneity. We learn that chaos is dangerous, and order is safety. We internalize that emotions must be managed, intuition ignored, and mystery avoided. As adults, this becomes a core operating system. We plan obsessively. We manage risk. We try to out-think, out-work, and out-perform our circumstances. We believe that if we can just get ahead of life, we'll finally feel at peace.

But control is never about peace. It's about fear. Fear of uncertainty. Fear of loss. Fear of vulnerability. Fear of death. And so, we create illusions of control, calendars, to-do lists, insurance plans, diets, schedules, not inherently bad, but often rooted in distrust. Distrust of the body. Distrust of others. Distrust of the universe. This mindset keeps us trapped in low vibration states. Anxiety becomes normalized. Tension becomes a lifestyle. The nervous system forgets how to rest.

—

The Illusion of Safety

Here is the truth we resist: There is no such thing as total safety in a dynamic world. Trying to control the uncontrollable only deepens suffering. Life is not a machine to be mastered. It is a mystery to be surrendered to. When we try to micromanage existence, we disconnect from flow. We stop listening. We stop trusting. We start grasping, defending, calculating. And we lose our magic.

Because the most powerful moments in life are the ones we did not plan. The love that arrives unexpectedly. The conversation that changes everything. The failure that leads to breakthrough. The silence that brings a message.

—

The Seduction of the Plan

Planning is not wrong. Strategy has its place. But when planning becomes a defense mechanism, it becomes a prison. We begin to live in the future, disconnected from the present. We obsess over how things should unfold, missing how they are. We project fear forward and call it preparation. But there's a difference between intention and attachment. Intention is rooted in trust. Attachment is rooted in fear.

Intention allows movement. Attachment demands outcomes. And when life inevitably veers from your script, attachment causes you to suffer.

—

What Control Costs Us

Control is not free. It costs us: Our presence: because we're always somewhere else mentally. Our relationships: because we begin to manipulate instead of connecting. Our creativity: because inspiration needs space. Our health: because the nervous system cannot heal when in constant defense. We become addicted to being right, to being prepared, to being protected. But real healing requires surrender. Real wisdom requires stillness. Real power requires openness.

—

The Body as a Teacher

Your body is one of the first places control manifests. You try to fix it, shape it, discipline it, deny it. But the body is not a machine. It is a messenger. It whispers what the mind refuses to admit. It breaks down when your alignment is lost. It holds the trauma your ego has buried. When you stop controlling your body and start listening to it, it becomes your ally. It tells you when to rest, when to act, when to let go. Surrendering to the body is not passivity. It is partnership.

—

The Myth of Manifestation Through Control

Many people encounter spiritual teachings and try to use them to reinforce control. They treat manifestation as a tool to manipulate the universe into giving them what they want. But true manifestation is not control, it is alignment. It is not about forcing reality to obey your will. It is about resonating so clearly with your truth that reality reshapes itself around your vibration. You don't manifest by fighting what is. You manifest by loving what is, and vibrating into what can be.

—

Moving From Force to Flow

—

The Tao of Surrender

In Taoist philosophy, there is a principle called *Wu Wei*, effortless action. It is not laziness. It is not indifference. It is the art of moving with the current instead of against it. It teaches us that the most powerful way to live is not through control, but through deep presence and listening. The river does not resist the stone. It curves around it. The tree does not hold its leaves in winter. It lets go.

Control says, "I must make this happen." Surrender says, "I will align with what wants to happen through me."

—

Trusting the Unknown

Surrender does not mean you abandon all agencies. It means you stop resisting what you cannot control. It means you trust that life has intelligence. That your soul has a plan. That your intuition knows more than your anxiety ever could. You begin to walk with life, not ahead of it. You begin to collaborate with the moment. You ask not, "How can I control this?" but "How can I respond with love, with wisdom, with presence?" You begin to trust the unknown, not because it is predictable, but because it is sacred.

—

Releasing the Fear of Losing Control

Underneath all control is a primal fear: If I don't hold everything together, everything will fall apart. But maybe what needs to fall apart is the illusion. You don't need to hold the universe together. That's not your job. Your job is to show up. To stay open. To remain aligned. When you release the grip, you realize: Life holds you. You were never carrying it. It was carrying you.

—

Reflection: The Power of Surrender

- Control is rooted in fear. Surrender is rooted in trust. You cannot force peace. You can only align with it. The universe does not respond to control. It responds to coherence. The more you let go, the more clearly life reflects your truth. Control creates resistance. Surrender creates flow. You were never meant to grip your way through life. You were meant to flow. To listen. To trust. And in that trust, you find your power.

—

—

Letting Go Is Not Giving Up

One of the greatest misconceptions is that letting go means failure. But letting go is not giving up. It is growing up. It is the moment when you stop trying to control reality and begin to co-create with it. Letting go means trusting that the universe is not working against you, but with you. It means acknowledging that your job is not to shape every outcome, but to respond to what is and create beauty from there. Letting go is not weakness. It is wisdom.

—

The Body as a Teacher

Control doesn't just live in the mind, it lives in the body. You can feel it in the clenched jaw, the tight shoulders, the shallow breath. The body remembers every time we tried to hold back, hold together, or hold it in. But the body is not trying to hurt you. It is trying to speak. When you stop trying to control the body and start listening to it, everything changes.

- Rest becomes sacred. Pleasure becomes permission. Breath becomes prayer. Surrendering to the body is surrendering to truth. It is remembering that the body is not a burden, it is a bridge.

—

Practical Ways to Loosen the Grip

If control is the habit, surrender must become the practice. Try these invitations: **Breathe** deeply and consciously when anxiety rises. **Write** your fears without censoring them. **Move** your body without choreography, let it be messy. **Trust** your first intuitive hit, not the overthought reaction. **Choose** love when fear begs for control. **Speak** truth even when you can't control the outcome. Each of these is an act of rebellion against the lie that you must have it all together. Each one is a crack in the illusion.

—

Presence: The End of Control

What control tries to give you, peace, clarity, alignment, already exists in presence. Presence is what remains when you stop trying to manage everything. In presence, you remember that nothing is truly wrong. That you are not behind. That this moment does not need to be fixed, it needs to be felt. And when you stop gripping, you begin receiving.

Chapter 3: The Birth of the Game

"To understand the dream, you must first understand the game. You must remember why you forgot."

In our previous journey together, we came to recognize this truth from the outside: life is a simulation, and the moment you remember you are its creator rather than merely its player, the entire experience shifts. But recognition alone is not transformation. This chapter goes deeper, not to re-teach what was already discovered, but to answer the question that recognition naturally raises: 'Why would a conscious, divine being choose to forget in the first place?' Understanding the design of the game is what allows you to play it with mastery rather than confusion.

Origins of the Divine Experiment

Imagine a canvas so vast that time itself has no boundary. A field of pure potential, unshaped and infinite, alive with intelligence and undivided awareness. This is not the beginning, because in truth, there is no beginning. But in the language of form, it is the closest approximation we have. From this eternal field, Source, God, the One, emerged the first impulse: to experience itself. Not as an idea, but as an unfolding. Not from observation, but through participation. The Absolute, by its very nature, had no contrast, no edges, no mirror. It was totality without reflection.

And so, the divine impulse fractured, not in violence, but in creativity. It divided the indivisible so it could see, feel, and remember itself. The Infinite dreamed limitation. Unity dreamed multiplicity. Eternity entered time. The unnamable gave birth to the first veil. This was the birth of the game.

—

Why We Chose to Forget

If we are divine, then why forget? Why fall into separation, limitation, and illusion? Because awakening has no meaning without forgetting. A sun does not know its brightness unless it is veiled. A soul cannot taste its courage unless it is tested. A god cannot embody compassion unless it feels suffering. To forget is not punishment. It is the catalyst for remembrance. We did not fall from grace. We dove into experience. We chose to wear masks, to clothe ourselves in time, to fragment into identities so we could gather our lost reflections and call that reunion love.

And so, the soul enters the game. It chooses a body, a timeline, a frequency. It downloads a personality, a family, a culture. It installs the veils: fear, doubt, ego, trauma. It joins the matrix. But even in the deepest amnesia, a thread remains, a golden tether back to Source. A whisper in the heart. A hunger in the spirit. A call to awaken.

—

The Structure of the Game

To navigate the dream, we must understand its rules, not in the way of enforcement, but of design. The Game, as we refer to it here, is a divine simulation: a matrix of experience where consciousness forgets itself so it can evolve, remember, and re-embody unity. It is not controlled by any one power or authority. It is a holographic construct maintained by mutual agreement.

The rules are simple: Everything is a reflection of your consciousness. Free will is absolute, but consequences are immediate or cumulative. Nothing happens to you; it happens for you. Resistance creates lessons. Acceptance creates momentum. Awakening is not escape, it is mastery. This world is not a trap. It is a training ground. The pain is not punishment. It is pressure that forges wisdom. The veil is not betrayal. It is the crucible of your evolution.

—

The Avatars We Wear

In the Game, you do not show up as your full light. That would defeat the purpose. You enter as an avatar: a body shaped by genes and memory. You pick up inherited beliefs, karmic threads, ancestral wounds. You take on a story and forget it's a script. You begin to believe:

- "I am this name."
- "I am these roles."
- "I am these traumas."

And the more immersed you become, the more real it all seems. But the avatar is not the player. It is the instrument. The interface. The mask. You are the consciousness behind the mask. The player behind the eyes. The presence behind the personality. And awakening is not the destruction of the avatar. It is the reclamation of the player.

—

The Matrix Within the Dream

The simulation has layers. The outer layer is the physical world, form, matter, experience. The inner layer is the matrix, belief, conditioning, fear, shame, scarcity. The Game becomes sticky when you believe the matrix is real. When you accept fear as fact. When you confuse the noise of the world with the voice of your soul. But the matrix only holds power if you agree to it.

The moment you question it; it begins to dissolve. The matrix says: You are small. You are separate. You must earn love. You are here to survive. But the soul remembers: I am infinite. I am connected. I am love. I am here to awaken.

—

Earth: A School for Souls

Some traditions say Earth is a prison planet. Others call it a battleground. But perhaps the most accurate metaphor is this: **Earth**

is a school. A sacred university for divine beings who wish to remember what they are, through the fire of forgetting. You enroll here knowing it won't be easy. You agree to certain challenges. You forget the plan so you can feel the full range of experience.

Pain becomes your teacher. Joy becomes your compass. Gratitude becomes your graduation. You do not fail here. You only repeat lessons until they are fully integrated.

—

The Players and the Program

Not everyone in the Game is awake. Not every being is sentient in the same way. Some are players. Some are programs. Some are guardians. Some are catalysts. There are background characters, what you might call NPCs (non-player characters), whose role is to provide context, contrast, or challenge. There are guides, seen and unseen, who gently steer you toward remembrance. And there are other souls, players like you, at different stages of the journey.

Your awakening may disturb them. Your light may trigger their shadow. But that, too, is part of the Game.

—

What It Means to Awaken in the Game

To awaken is not to escape the Game. It is to become lucid within it. You begin to notice synchronicities. You start to see the repeating numbers, the mirrored conversations, the patterns you couldn't see before. You become the observer. You begin to respond rather than react. You start to feel the edges of your old identity soften. Awakening is not an event. It is a frequency. And once you tune into it, the world reorganizes around it.

Your dreams change. Your relationships shift. Your desires evolve. And the rules of the Game begin to feel less restrictive, not because they've changed, but because you're playing at a new level.

—

When the Game No Longer Feels Like a Game

There will come a point when it all feels too much. The pain. The loss. The confusion. You will want to exit. You will wonder why you ever chose this. You will forget that you are more than the role. This is the threshold. The edge of remembrance. The final test before lucidity. Do not despair. You are not failing. You are feeling the friction of your own expansion.

Breathe. Trust. Remember. You are not here to win the Game. You are here to **wake up inside it**.

Reflection: You Are the Player

- The Game is a divine simulation, a field of forgetting and remembrance. You chose to enter, to evolve, to experience. Your avatar is not your essence. The matrix is a layer of illusion, not reality. Awakening begins when you stop identifying with the program. You are not trapped, you are training. And when you remember the rules, the illusion no longer binds you. You begin to move with grace. You begin to choose with clarity. You begin to live with purpose.

The Game is not your enemy. It is your mirror. It is your masterpiece. It is your great forgetting, in service of your greatest remembering. Now, you step onto the field not as a victim, but as a lucid player. The Game continues. But now... you remember who you are.

Chapter 4: The Veil of Forgetting

"You are not learning something new. You are remembering something eternal."

The Descent into Forgetting

Before you took form, you knew who you were. You were aware of your connection to Source. You were whole, radiant, and timeless. There was no fear, no separation, no loss. But you wanted to experience that truth, not just know it. You wanted to remember what it meant to be divine through the lens of limitation. So, you chose to forget. This forgetting is not a flaw in the human condition. It is the very structure of the human journey. Like a pearl forming inside the shell, your brilliance could only be refined by the friction of density. You entered this life through a sacred veil, a fog that blurred your knowing, so you could rediscover it as truth.

The veil is not a punishment. It is a purpose. You did not lose yourself. You chose to hide in plain sight.

—

The Layers of the Veil

The veil of forgetting is not a single moment of amnesia, it is layered, interwoven through every aspect of being. **1. The Physical Veil**: Upon birth, your nervous system is flooded with sensation. Your awareness shifts from vast unity to localized experience. You begin to identify with your body, your senses, and the stimuli around you. The world becomes overwhelming and vivid. To cope, you narrow your focus. You begin to forget.

2. The Emotional Veil: As you grow, your emotions are shaped by family, environment, and culture. You're taught to suppress, to deny, to perform. Emotional pain becomes an armor that shields you from truth. You begin to internalize shame, fear, unworthiness. You forget your intrinsic value. **3. The Mental Veil**: Language reinforces division. You are told you are separate, separate from others, from nature, from God. You learn to label, to judge, to compartmentalize.

The mind becomes dominant, and intuition fades into the background. You forget your connection to all things.

4. The Spiritual Veil: Religious systems offer glimpses of truth, but often cloak it in dogmatic fear, hierarchy, or external authority. You are told salvation lies elsewhere, in the sky, in the future, in someone else's hands. The inner flame dims under the weight of dogma. You forget you are the divine. Each veil is a program. Each program shapes your perception. And the more you identify with these layers, the more asleep you become to what lies beneath them.

The Purpose of Amnesia

Why would a soul choose to forget? Because the soul values depth. Because remembrance is more powerful than possession. To know something from the inside out is to truly embody it. To awaken in the dark is to become the light. Forgetting allows you to fall in love with truth again. It allows you to choose presence over programming. It allows you to rebuild the bridge from illusion to divinity, and in doing so, to become more than a witness of light. You become its vessel.

This is not suffering for suffering's sake. This is soul-alchemy. Every moment of pain, confusion, and loss is the friction that refines your clarity. Every fall into illusion is a setup for a breakthrough of remembrance. You didn't come to earth to escape illusion. You came to master it.

–

Signs of Awakening from the Veil

At first, the veil is total. You play your roles, pursue your goals, repeat your patterns. But eventually, something begins to crack through. A recurring dream. A déjà vu. A longing you can't name. A sudden moment of stillness, where everything feels holy. A loss that breaks you open. A question that refuses to be silenced: "Is this all there is?" These are the openings in the veil, the glitch in the program. They are not signs of breakdown. They are invitations.

Your soul is knocking. Your true self is surfacing. You begin to question what once felt normal. You feel the discomfort of inauthenticity. You start to crave silence, solitude, simplicity. You begin to see life not as random, but symbolic. This is the veil beginning to thin. And once it does, nothing can be unseen.

Remembering Through Contrast

Contrast is the curriculum of this world. You understand truth by first believing the lie. You know love by having felt its absence. You find wholeness by walking through fragmentation. Contrast is not your enemy; it is your compass. Each painful emotion is not a failure. It is a message. Anger shows you where your boundaries have been crossed. Sadness shows you where love was lost.

- Anxiety shows you where presence is missing. These are not blocks. They are breadcrumbs. Follow them, and they lead you home.

The Role of Pain in Peeling the Veil

Pain, in this reality, is sacred. Not because it is good, but because it is clarifying. Pain peels away illusion. It breaks the shell of ego. It demands attention. And in that raw, honest space, something eternal stirs. Many people awaken through suffering, not because it's required, but because pain demands presence. It interrupts the trance. It says: "Look here. Feel this. Something isn't aligned."

Pain is the fire that burns through the fog. It leaves you naked but cleansed. And in the ashes, you find the glowing coals of truth.

The Reclamation of Memory

The process of awakening is not about becoming something new. It is about remembering what was always true. You remember that you are not your thoughts. You remember that your worth is not conditional. You remember that the divine is not elsewhere. It's not a single moment. It's a cascade of moments, each one clearing away the fog. A sunset that moves you to tears.

- A child's laugh that breaks your cynicism. A silent knowing that arises in meditation. You remember through experience, not belief. You remember by feeling the truth in your bones. And the more you remember, the lighter the veil becomes.

Why Some Stay Asleep

You may wonder: why don't others see what I see? Because not all souls are ready. Because the veil is comforting to some. Because awakening demands courage, and not everyone is prepared to lose who they thought they were. Let them be. Your job is not to rip the veil from others. It is to gently lift your own, and let your life become a mirror.

Your presence is the invitation. Your peace is the protest. Your light is the signal. And when they are ready, they too will begin to see.

Practical Tools for Lifting the Veil

1. **Meditation**: Stillness quiets the noise of the mind. In that quiet, truth speaks. **Breathwork**: Conscious breathing restores presence and opens inner awareness. **Dream Journaling**: Dreams are messages from the soul. Recording them accelerates remembrance. **Self-Inquiry**: Ask, "Who am I?" and follow the question beyond identity. **Nature Immersion**: Nature is a mirror without distortion. It reminds you of your essence. **Service**: Acts of compassion anchor the soul in unity.
2. **Shadow Work**: Explore the repressed parts of you. Behind every shadow is power. Each of these tools thins the veil by bringing you closer to presence.

Reflection: The Return Begins

- You did not fall, you descended with purpose. Forgetting was not failure, it was setup for transformation. The veil is not your enemy, it is your training ground. The pain you carry is the key to your remembrance. Awakening is not becoming, it is returning. You are not broken. You are buried. And the veil is beginning to lift. Welcome back.

And having crossed back through the veil, you find yourself standing inside something larger than memory, the great spiraling pattern of creation that has been cycling since before time had a name.

Chapter 5: The Eternal Return: Creation, Collapse, and Cosmic Memory

"Nothing is lost in the cosmos. What ends becomes the seed of what begins."

To the unawakened, time appears as a straight line, a path from birth to death, from creation to final judgment. But to the mystic, the seer, the ancient soul, time reveals its truer form: a wheel, ever-turning. This wheel, known to some as the Ouroboros, to others as the Yuga cycle, and to still others as the rhythm of samsara, spins not aimlessly, but with purpose, guiding all creation through birth, decay, destruction, and renewal. In this chapter, we turn our attention to this universal pulse: the cosmic rhythm of the eternal return.

The Illusion of Linear Time

Modern society is built upon a linear understanding of time. We are taught to believe in a beginning (the Big Bang, birth), a middle (life, civilization), and an end (death, apocalypse, heat death). Progress is measured in forward motion. History is thought of as a ladder or a timeline. But ancient cosmologies and metaphysical systems tell a different story. Time, in their view, is not a one-way street but a **circle**, or more accurately, a **spiral**, ever-returning, yet never quite the same. It is this spiral that holds the secret of both the universe and our inner world. Each rotation brings us closer to remembrance, if we are awake enough to perceive it.

Mythologies of Cycles

Across the world's traditions, creation myths do not simply begin and end, they repeat. They unfold in patterns that mirror one another, whether among the mountains of India, the deserts of Mesopotamia, or the forests of Northern Europe. Let us revisit the myths not as isolated tales, but as **echoes of a shared cosmic memory**. In Hinduism, the four Yugas (Satya, Treta, Dvapara, and Kali) represent the declining moral ages of the universe. In the Satya Yuga, truth and virtue reign; in Kali Yuga, darkness and illusion dominate. At the end of Kali, the world is destroyed and recreated, beginning a new cycle.

In **Norse mythology**, the gods face Ragnarok, a final battle of destruction. Fire consumes the earth. But afterward, a new world rises from the sea, and life begins again. In **Greek cosmology**, the Five Ages of Man, Golden, Silver, Bronze, Heroic, and Iron, devolve into increasing corruption, ending in collapse and rebirth. **Mayan** and **Aztec** cultures believed we are living in the Fifth Sun, the fifth world, preceded by four destroyed ones. Flood, fire, wind, and jaguars consumed the earlier creations. Now we stand on the precipice of the next destruction.

Even in the **Bible**, though time is often read as linear, cycles persist. The Garden leads to the Fall, which leads to destruction (flood), and then covenant, exile, return, and messianic hope. It is a cycle of divine creation and human forgetting, followed by redemption and renewal.

The Pattern: From Chaos to Order and Back Again

Each of these stories follows the same archetypal structure: **Primordial Chaos**: a void, abyss, or darkness from which creation springs. **Divine Ordering**: gods or forces separate sky from earth, light from dark. **Creation of Man**: often from clay, dust, or divine breath. **The Fall or Decline**: pride, disobedience, or corruption leads to imbalance. **Destruction or Collapse**: flood, fire, war, or forgetfulness resets the cycle.

1. **Rebirth**: a remnant survives; a seed is planted; a new age begins. This is not merely allegorical. It is metaphysical. These cycles represent the **heartbeat of the cosmos**, a rhythm present in galaxies, societies, and the very breath of human experience. Everything evolves, and everything resets.

Time as a Spiral: The Path to Awakening

If time were a circle, we'd be trapped in eternal repetition. But the great teachers have shown us that time moves in spirals. The cycle returns, but not to the same point, it returns to **deepen awareness**. This is seen in **Buddhism's wheel of samsara**, the soul reincarnates endlessly until it awakens and breaks the cycle. In **Gnostic teachings**, the divine spark is trapped in matter and forgets its origin; only through gnosis (knowing) can it ascend.

The **Ouroboros**, the serpent eating its own tail, is not consuming itself in futility. It is **transforming**, purifying, alchemizing its own nature. Each life, each age, each generation repeats the great cosmic themes, but with the possibility of awakening within the pattern.

Why the Cycle? The Metaphysical Purpose

Why would a divine intelligence design a universe to loop endlessly through creation and destruction? The answer lies in the nature of consciousness itself. Creation is not a final product. It is a **process of becoming**. Through cycles, the One experiences multiplicity. Through forgetting, it remembers more deeply. Through descent, it discovers the strength to rise. **The cycle exists to refine awareness.** Just as a soul reincarnates to learn lessons it did not grasp before, the universe reincarnates to **reflect on itself more clearly**. Each Yuga, each world, each aeon is a chapter in the journey of Divine Self-Discovery.

In **Hindu Vedanta**, this is called *Lila*, the divine play. In **Buddhism**, it is illusion (*Maya*) to be transcended. In **Gnosticism**, it is the prison to escape. Yet all agree: the purpose is not to remain in the loop, but to **wake up inside it**.

Modern Echoes: Science, Simulation, and Psychology

Even modern frameworks unknowingly echo ancient truths. Cosmologists propose the universe began with a **Big Bang**, a singularity exploding into time and space. But now some suggest a **Big Bounce** may follow, a collapse into a singularity and a new expansion, repeating forever. **Simulation theory** posits we may be inside a programmed reality, a loop designed to test and evolve consciousness. **Quantum physics** shows that particles exist in states of potential until observed, mirroring creation through divine awareness.

Psychologically, we repeat cycles too. Trauma, relationships, self-sabotage, they loop until we learn. **Carl Jung** said: *"Until you make the unconscious conscious, it will direct your life and you will call it fate."* The eternal return is not just cosmic, it is **intensely personal**.

Breaking the Loop: Becoming the Dreamer

So how do we escape the wheel? Not by force. Not by denial. But by **waking up**. To see the pattern is to weaken its grip. To accept the cycle is to move beyond it. Awareness is the liberator. Once we recognize that we are **not the story**, but the **witness of the story**, we shift roles, from character to author, from dreamer to awakened Self.

The myths are not simply old tales, they are **maps**. They remind us that fall leads to rise, that death begets life, and that even in the darkest hour of the Kali Yuga, a light remains, hidden in the ashes, waiting to ignite the next dawn.

Final Reflection: The Memory of the Stars

Everything we are, everything we do, has happened before. And yet, it is all new. The ancients remembered something we have forgotten: that life is not a random line drawn across time, but a **dance**, a **symphony**, a **dream of awakening**. In that dream, we fall. We break. We forget. But always, we return. Not to the beginning, but to the beginning made new, infused with all we have learned.

"The dream repeats, not because you are cursed, but because the soul is trying to sing a song it once knew by heart."

This is the gift of the eternal return. Not punishment. Not prison. But **possibility.** When you awaken, even the loop becomes a ladder. And then you will see: you were never walking in circles. You were spiraling toward the stars.

Chapter 6: Meaning or Mistake? Exploring the Nature of Existence

"What if the absence of meaning is not a flaw, but the point?"

The Question That Echoes Through Eternity

Why are we here? It is perhaps the oldest question ever asked: whispered in caves, written in sacred texts, debated in universities, and pondered in the quiet solitude of sleepless nights. It is the question that refuses to die, no matter how advanced our science becomes or how complex our philosophies grow. Is existence a cosmic accident, the result of random interactions in an indifferent universe? Or is it intentional, designed, and meaningful beyond our current capacity to comprehend?

The tension between these possibilities is not merely intellectual; it is deeply personal. It shapes how we love, how we suffer, how we hope, and how we endure. Some conclude that life is nothing more than a biological anomaly, a fleeting spark in an otherwise lifeless void. Others feel, with an unshakable certainty, that something profound is unfolding beneath the surface of reality: something purposeful, something sacred. This chapter does not seek to force a single answer. Instead, it invites you to explore the full spectrum of possibility, from the stark emptiness of nihilism to the luminous interconnectedness of a conscious cosmos, and beyond. Because perhaps the truth is not found at one extreme, but in the space that holds them all.

The Void of Nihilism

Nihilism stands as one of the most intellectually honest conclusions a purely materialist worldview can produce. If the universe is composed only of matter and energy, governed by blind physical laws, then meaning does not exist as an inherent property of reality. It is not written into the fabric of the cosmos. It is not waiting to be discovered like a hidden treasure; it is simply absent. From this perspective, the universe is vast, silent, and indifferent. Stars are born and die without intention. Galaxies collide without purpose. Life emerges not because it was meant to, but because conditions happened to allow it.

You are here because of chance: because atoms assembled in a way that allowed for self-replication, because evolution favored survival over extinction, because time and probability permitted your existence. There is no grand narrative, no cosmic author, no predetermined meaning: only existence. And yet, something about this conclusion feels incomplete. Not incorrect, but unfinished. Because if meaning is truly absent, why does the human mind relentlessly seek it? Why does the heart resist the idea that love is merely a chemical reaction? Why do moments of beauty, connection, and transcendence feel so undeniably significant? Nihilism explains the mechanics of existence, but it struggles to account for the experience of it. It tells us how things happen, but not why it matters that they do. And perhaps that is its ultimate limitation.

The Hunger That Cannot Be Ignored

The search for meaning is not a defect in human cognition; it is not a glitch in the system, but a signal. From the moment we become self-aware, we begin to ask questions that have no immediate survival value. We wonder about purpose, about destiny, about the nature of existence itself. This curiosity does not help us hunt. It does not directly aid reproduction. And yet it persists across every culture, every era, every civilization that has ever existed. Because the need for meaning is not an evolutionary accident; it is a defining feature of consciousness itself.

We seek meaning in everything: in relationships, in suffering, in success, in failure. We attempt to weave narratives that transform random events into coherent stories. Even in the face of tragedy, the question arises: what does this mean? This question emerges not from weakness, but from depth. It suggests that somewhere within us is an awareness that refuses to accept emptiness as the final answer. And so we are left with a paradox: the universe appears indifferent, yet we feel that it matters. This tension is not something to resolve. It is something to explore.

A Conscious Universe: The Living Fabric of Reality

What if the universe is not indifferent at all? What if the assumption of lifelessness is the illusion? Panpsychism offers a radically different perspective, suggesting that consciousness is not something that emerges from complexity, but something that exists at the most fundamental level of reality. In this view, consciousness is not produced by the brain; the brain is simply a receiver, a translator, a filter through which consciousness expresses itself. Every particle, every field, every aspect of existence carries with it a rudimentary form of awareness, not awareness as we experience it, but a primitive, intrinsic quality of being that underlies all matter.

This idea, once dismissed as purely philosophical, is gaining renewed attention due to anomalies in modern physics. Experiments have shown that particles behave differently when observed, as though awareness itself influences physical outcomes. Entangled particles appear to communicate across vast distances instantaneously, defying classical explanations. These phenomena challenge the assumption that consciousness is separate from the physical world and hint instead that consciousness may be woven into the very structure of reality. If this is true, then nothing is truly inert, nothing is meaningless, and your existence is not a random occurrence within a dead universe; it is an expression of a living, conscious whole.

The Simulation Hypothesis: Reality as Experience

Another perspective emerges from the intersection of technology and philosophy. What if reality is not base-level existence, but a constructed experience? Simulation theory proposes that what we perceive as reality could be a highly advanced, immersive environment, not necessarily artificial in the way we conventionally understand it, but structured, governed by rules, and designed for interaction. This is not about trivializing existence as a game, but about reframing it entirely.

Consider the parallels. In a video game, there are rules, boundaries, and objectives. The environment feels real to the player while they are immersed within it. The character they control is not who they are, but an avatar through which they experience the world. Now imagine that consciousness itself is the player, the body is the avatar, the mind is the interface, and life is the experience. Within this framework, challenges are not punishments; they are opportunities for growth. Obstacles are not random; they are part of the design. Awakening occurs when the player begins to recognize that they are not limited to the character they are playing. This does not diminish meaning. It transforms it. Because meaning is no longer something imposed from outside; it is something discovered through engagement.

The Gnostic Memory: A Forgotten Origin

Long before modern science and technology, ancient traditions spoke of a deeper truth hidden beneath the surface of reality. Gnostic philosophy suggests that we are not merely physical beings, but fragments of a greater divine source, temporarily immersed in a material world that obscures our true nature. In this narrative, existence is not a mistake, but a descent, a forgetting. The world is not necessarily evil, but it is incomplete. It is a veil that limits perception, creating the illusion of separation. And within each of us is a quiet knowing, a subtle intuition that whispers: there is more than this.

This manifests as a sense of longing: a feeling of not quite belonging, a desire for something we cannot fully articulate. It is the spiritual restlessness that drives the seeker, the mystic, the philosopher who cannot settle for surface explanations. Gnosticism does not ask us to reject the world, but to see through it, to recognize that what we perceive is not the entirety of what is. Awakening, in this tradition, is not about escaping reality. It is about remembering our place within it.

The Harmony of Opposites

At first glance, these perspectives appear contradictory. Nihilism denies inherent meaning. Panpsychism affirms universal consciousness. Simulation theory reframes reality as structured experience. Gnosticism speaks of divine origin and forgetfulness. But what if they are not mutually exclusive? What if they are different lenses through which the same truth can be observed? What if the universe appears meaningless precisely so that we are free to create meaning; everything is conscious, but we experience separation in order to learn unity; we are both the player and the character; and the fall into matter is not a failure, but a necessary step toward awakening?

The human mind seeks consistency. It wants a single, definitive answer. But reality may not operate within such constraints. It may be layered, paradoxical, and multidimensional. Our task is not to simplify it, but to expand our capacity to hold it: to become comfortable with the mystery, and to find that the mystery itself is the invitation.

The Role of Conscious Participation

One idea begins to emerge clearly from this exploration: reality is not something that simply happens to you. It is something you participate in. Your attention, your perception, your interpretation all influence how reality is experienced. You do not merely observe the world; you engage with it, shape it, and give it texture through the quality of your presence. The question then shifts from 'Is there meaning?' to 'What meaning am I creating?' This is not about denying hardship or pretending that everything is positive. It is about recognizing that interpretation transforms experience. The same event can be seen as a failure or a lesson, as an ending or a beginning. And in that choice, reality changes, not externally, but internally. And the internal world is where meaning lives.

The Alchemy of Interpretation

To choose meaning is not to ignore pain; it is to transform it. Suffering, in its raw form, is often chaotic and overwhelming. But when meaning is applied, it becomes something else: a teacher, a catalyst, a turning point. A broken relationship becomes an opportunity to understand oneself more deeply. A loss becomes a doorway to compassion. A failure becomes a redirection toward something more aligned with your authentic path. This is not naive optimism. It is conscious interpretation: the recognition that while we may not control every event, we have the capacity to shape how those events define us. This is the essence of emotional alchemy: the ability to transmute raw experience into wisdom and growth.

Freedom Within Structure

A common concern arises when considering the possibility that reality is designed or structured: do we have free will? The answer lies in understanding the nature of freedom itself. Freedom is not absolute control over all circumstances; it is not the ability to dictate every outcome. Instead, it is the capacity to choose how we respond. You may not control the conditions of your birth or determine every challenge you face. But within those conditions, you have choice. You choose your perspective, your actions, your direction. And those choices ripple outward, influencing the trajectory of your life in ways far greater than they may appear in any single moment. Free will is not about controlling the entire game. It is about how fully and consciously you play it.

The Dissolution of the Question

As awareness deepens, something subtle begins to shift. The need to define meaning starts to fade, not because meaning disappears, but because it becomes inherent. You no longer need a reason to appreciate beauty. You no longer require justification to love. You no longer seek external validation for simply being. Life is experienced directly, without the constant need for explanation. This is not apathy; it is presence. A state in which existence is sufficient in and of itself. And in this state, the question 'What is the meaning of life?' loses its urgency, because life is no longer something to be explained. It is something to be lived.

Remembering the Creator Within

To remember is not to uncover a single, ultimate truth. It is to recognize your role in the unfolding of reality. You are not separate from existence; you are an expression of it. Meaning is not something that exists independently of you. It is something that arises through you, through your choices, your awareness, and your engagement with the world. You are not here to passively observe life. You are here to participate in its creation: to shape it, to experience it, to give it meaning through the quality of your attention and the sincerity of your becoming. You are not an accident. You are an artist. And life is your canvas.

Reflection: The Mirror of Meaning

Nihilism reveals the absence of imposed meaning, stripping away illusion and forcing us to confront the void with intellectual honesty. Panpsychism restores the sense of aliveness, suggesting that consciousness permeates all things and that nothing in existence is truly inert. Simulation theory reframes existence as an interactive experience, inviting participation and discovery rather than passive endurance. Gnosticism reminds us of a deeper origin, a truth that lies beyond appearances and calls us to remember what we have always been. Each perspective offers a piece of the puzzle. But none of them, on their own, are complete. Because the final piece is you: your awareness, your interpretation, your choice. Meaning is not given. It is created. And in that creation, something extraordinary happens: the observer becomes the participant, the participant becomes the creator, and the creator begins to awaken.

Chapter 7: The Illusion of Free Will

There comes a moment in many lives when the underlying logic of choice begins to feel uncertain. Not because opportunities disappear, but because patterns persist regardless of how thoughtfully one chooses. Plans unravel despite careful execution. Relationships replay familiar themes wearing different faces. Lessons return with quiet insistence. What once felt like freedom of will slowly begins to reveal itself as something more constrained, or more mysterious, than it appeared.

At first, this is deeply unsettling. Most of us are raised to believe that life responds directly to effort, that correct decisions lead to favorable outcomes and mistakes lead to failure. When life does not obey this logic, we assume we have misunderstood the rules. We search for better strategies, better beliefs, better techniques. We try to regain control. Even spirituality often reinforces this impulse. We are told that if we meditate correctly, visualize clearly, or align our thoughts properly, we can steer reality toward preferred outcomes. Difficulty, in this framework, is evidence of misalignment. Suffering becomes a problem to solve rather than an experience to enter.

Yet beneath the exhaustion of constant striving, a quieter question begins to surface, one that rarely receives language: *What if life is not resisting me because I am doing something wrong? What if it is resisting me because I am trying to interfere with something already in motion?* This chapter explores that possibility.

Incarnation as Deliberate Immersion

Within the metaphysics of the Dream, incarnation is not accidental. It is not a test imposed by an external authority, nor a punishment for past actions. It is a voluntary immersion, chosen by consciousness itself. Before identity, memory, and narrative arise, there exists a level of awareness that does not experience time sequentially. From that vantage point, life is not encountered as a series of moments but as a complete landscape of potential experiences. Joy and grief, power and helplessness, certainty and collapse, all are visible as textures within a single field.

From this perspective, a life is not designed as a list of events but as an experiential arc, a trajectory of deepening states of consciousness that can only be understood by moving through them. Certain states of being must be lived in order to be known. Certain encounters must be entered fully, not understood conceptually or avoided through strategy. The purpose of incarnation, then, is not achievement. It is **exposure.**

Love is not meant to be theorized, it must be felt in its vulnerability. Loss is not meant to be bypassed, it must be entered until it dissolves resistance. Identity must be built so it can later fracture. Certainty must arise so that doubt can undo it. These experiences are not chosen moment by moment by the human self. They arise because they were selected *before* the human self existed.

From within the Dream, this feels like fate. From the perspective of the higher self, it is authorship.

Predestination Reconsidered

The idea of predestination often provokes discomfort because it is associated with coercion, the sense that life is dictated by forces beyond one's control. But predestination only feels oppressive when the author is imagined as *other*. When the author is **you**, the entire meaning changes. Predestination, in this framework, does not mean that every event is fixed in detail. It means that **certain experiences are non-negotiable**. They form the structural spine of the incarnation. You may encounter them early or late, gently or violently, consciously or unconsciously, but you will encounter them.

This explains why people often spend years avoiding a truth only to meet it again under harsher conditions. It explains why relationships repeat the same emotional pattern despite changing partners. It explains why careers, identities, and belief systems collapse at precisely the moment they seem most secure. Life is not correcting you.

It is **returning you to yourself**.

The Birth of Flux

Once embodied, consciousness forgets its authorship. This forgetting is not a flaw, it is a requirement. Without it, experience would lose its immediacy. The Dream would feel staged rather than lived. But forgetting introduces friction. The ego, formed within the Dream, becomes invested in comfort, safety, coherence, and identity preservation. It measures success by stability and control rather than by depth of experience. When life introduces discomfort, uncertainty, or emotional exposure, the ego interprets it as error.

And so it intervenes. It plans, manipulates, manifests, and strategizes. It attempts to reroute the unfolding toward outcomes it believes will provide security or validation. This intervention is not wrong, but it is **misaligned**. The resulting tension can be understood as *flux*. Flux is the turbulence created when the ego's agenda diverges from the deeper experiential trajectory. It manifests as resistance, repetition, emotional strain, and the sense of being pushed back onto a path one is trying to avoid.

Traditions have called this karma.

Karma as Reconciliation

In popular culture, karma is often framed as reward and punishment. Good actions are believed to produce favorable outcomes; bad actions produce suffering. This moral interpretation misses the deeper mechanism at work. Karma is not judgment.

It is **reconciliation**.

If an incarnation is designed to experience abandonment, then abandonment will recur until it is fully lived, not resolved, not healed, not transcended, but *felt*. If power is part of the arc, authority will appear again and again until its psychological impact is integrated. Avoidance does not cancel these experiences. It delays them. Distorts them. Intensifies them. This is why suffering escalates when ignored. The universe is not being cruel. It is being precise. The greater the resistance, the greater the force required to bring the experience into awareness.

Life is not asking you to behave better. It is asking you to **stop running**.

Spirituality and the Illusion of Control

Here, the role of spirituality becomes paradoxical. Meditation, manifestation, visualization, and affirmation are often presented as tools of liberation, methods to transcend suffering or engineer reality. While they can regulate emotion and quiet the mind, they frequently reinforce a deeper illusion: that the ego is meant to direct the unfolding of life. When spirituality becomes a strategy for control, it turns into another form of resistance. The seeker attempts to rise above experiences that were meant to be entered fully. Difficulty is framed as failure rather than invitation.

This explains why spiritual effort often leads to frustration. The more one tries to "align," the more life seems to push back. The more one attempts to manifest ease, the more complexity appears. This does not mean spiritual practices are useless. It means their purpose is misunderstood. They are not exits from the Dream. They are **conditioning mechanisms** that preserve immersion while softening the intensity of experience.

When mistaken for tools of authorship, they prolong struggle rather than resolve it.

Free Will as Interface

So where does free will fit into this model? Free will exists, but not at the level we have been taught to imagine. It does not operate as authorship over the structure of life. It operates as agency over **interpretation**. You are free to choose: how you relate to what is happening how long you resist it how deeply you engage with it how much meaning you extract from it

You are not free to opt out of the core experiences you designed. Free will governs **timing**, not destination. It determines how long you wrestle with an experience before allowing it to complete itself. This is why life feels both inevitable and deeply personal. Events feel scripted, yet reactions feel spontaneous. Both perceptions are accurate within their respective layers. The belief in free will serves a crucial function. It preserves immersion. Without it, incarnation would collapse into spectatorship. The sensation of agency allows experiences to feel real rather than symbolic.

Awakening as Recognition, Not Escape

Awakening, in this framework, is not the realization that nothing matters. It is the recognition that **everything matters because it was chosen**. Not chosen by the ego, but by the deeper self that entered the Dream knowingly. This recognition does not end action. It transforms it. Decisions still arise. Choices still occur. But they no longer carry the weight of self-justification. Outcomes are met with curiosity rather than defense.

Resistance softens. Karma loosens. Repetition loses its force. Not because lessons disappear, but because they are no longer resisted.

Cooperation with the Path

When the illusion of control dissolves, life does not become passive. It becomes fluid. Movement continues, but without friction. Effort gives way to participation. Struggle gives way to cooperation. This is not resignation. It is alignment across time. You stop pulling against yourself. And in that moment, a quieter freedom appears, not the freedom to change the path, but the freedom to walk it without resistance.

Closing Reflection

You were never meant to control your life. You were meant to experience the life you already designed. Free will was never the power to rewrite the story. It was the sensation of choosing how long you forget that you wrote it. And when remembering begins, not as memory, but as recognition, the Dream does not end. It deepens. Once the illusion of control begins to loosen, a new and unsettling question arises. If life is not meant to be managed, forced, or overridden, if resistance itself is the source of friction, then how is one meant to live? What replaces striving when the will is no longer trying to dominate the unfolding? This is the threshold where understanding alone becomes insufficient. Recognition must give way to practice. Not the practice of control, but the practice of cooperation. What follows is not withdrawal from life, nor passive surrender, but the discovery of a subtler form of participation, one that moves with the current rather than against it. This is the art of allowance.

Chapter 8: The Art of Allowance: Freedom Beyond Control

There comes a moment in every life when effort begins to feel strangely counterproductive. The harder one tries to steer events, the more resistance seems to arise. Doors refuse to open. Circumstances repeat. The same emotional patterns resurface in different relationships, careers, and inner dialogues. Lessons return wearing new disguises, as if reality itself were recycling unresolved themes. What once felt like agency, choice, discipline, intention, slowly reveals itself as strain.

At first, this feels disorienting. We are taught that effort is synonymous with progress. If something is not working, the answer must be to try harder, refine the method, or search for a better strategy. And yet, here, effort appears to deepen the problem. Control tightens, but clarity recedes. This moment is often misread as failure. It is not. It is an invitation. It is the point at which the architecture of the Dream begins to reveal a deeper logic, one that does not respond to force, but to alignment.

Most of us are trained, from childhood onward, to believe that life is something to be managed. We are conditioned to see the world as a system that must be navigated correctly to avoid pain and maximize reward. Success is framed as the result of proper decisions, sufficient discipline, and relentless self-improvement. Failure is framed as error, weakness, or poor execution. Even our most intimate philosophies tend to echo this assumption: that fulfillment arrives when we finally figure life out.

Spirituality, which claims to liberate us from suffering, often reinforces the same model. We are told that if we meditate correctly, visualize clearly, manifest skillfully, or raise our vibration high enough, reality will bend to our will. Awakening becomes another project. Enlightenment becomes another achievement. Inner peace becomes another outcome to be engineered. Beneath all of this lies a shared, largely unquestioned assumption: That the individual self is meant to direct the unfolding of life.

But what if this assumption is false? What if the deeper truth is that life is not waiting to be commanded, but to be received? In the metaphysics of the Dream, incarnation is not a blank slate. It is not a random assignment nor a test imposed by an external authority. It is an intentional entry into a sequence, an arc of experience chosen before memory, before identity, before the sense of "I" emerged within time. This sequence is not a rigid script of events, but a landscape of encounters: moments of love and loss, power and vulnerability, clarity and confusion. These experiences are not selected to reward or punish, but to expose consciousness to aspects of itself that cannot be known from a distance.

The higher self, the self beyond time, does not design outcomes. It designs encounters. Outcomes are secondary. What matters is what is *met*, what is *felt*, what is *integrated.* From that vantage point, suffering is not an error, and pleasure is not a goal. Both are textures through which awareness deepens. But how can an encounter carry its full emotional weight if one already knows the ending? For this design to work, it must be forgotten.

If one entered life with full memory intact, experience would lose its weight. Pain would be symbolic rather than visceral. Surprise would evaporate. Choice would feel theatrical rather than real. Meaning would collapse into abstraction. Forgetting is not a flaw in the system, it is the mechanism that allows experience to be immersive. The veil of forgetting is what makes life feel consequential. But forgetting comes with a cost. Without awareness of the deeper design, the incarnated self assumes it must take responsibility for navigation. It confuses participation with authorship. It assumes that discomfort means something has gone wrong, that resistance signals deviation, that difficulty is evidence of failure. And so it begins to interfere.

This interference is not malicious. It is protective. Control arises as a coping strategy within uncertainty. The ego does not seek dominance; it seeks stability. It attempts to minimize pain, predict outcomes, and secure identity. In doing so, it adopts a posture of management toward life. This is the birth of control. At first, control appears functional. It helps the self adapt, survive, and organize experience. But over time, it becomes constrictive. It narrows perception. It turns life into a problem to be solved rather than a process to be lived. It demands that reality conform to expectation.

When reality does not comply, tension arises. This tension is what ancient traditions named karma. Karma, in the metaphysics of the Dream, is neither punishment nor reward. It is feedback. It is the system re-presenting an experience until it is met without resistance. When an experience is avoided, denied, or distorted, it does not disappear, it returns in altered form. The pattern repeats not because the universe is cruel, but because the lesson remains incomplete.

Karma persists only as long as resistance persists. This is why the same relational dynamics recur across different partners. Why the same emotional wounds surface in new contexts. Why the same themes echo through different chapters of life. The forms change, but the essence remains. The system is not judging the individual; it is inviting completion. An experience resisted must return. An experience allowed can dissolve.

Here, the concept of "letting go" enters, and is almost always misunderstood. Letting go is commonly mistaken for passivity, resignation, or disengagement. It is framed as withdrawal from life, as if allowance means surrendering agency or abandoning responsibility. This misunderstanding has caused more harm than perhaps any other spiritual misinterpretation. Letting go is not abdication. It is the relinquishment of a false role. To let go is not to stop acting; it is to stop *interfering*. It is the release of the belief that one must control the timing, form, and arrival of experience. It is the recognition that life does not need to be forced, it needs to be met.

Allowance is not weakness. It is alignment. When one allows experience to arrive, rather than attempting to engineer it, something subtle but profound shifts. Life is no longer perceived as an adversary. Events lose their antagonistic tone. Even difficulty arrives with a strange sense of familiarity, not because it is pleasant, but because it belongs. Life ceases to feel like a test one might fail and begins to feel like a conversation one is already part of.

This does not render the individual inert. Action still occurs. Choices are still made. But they arise from a different place. Instead of being driven by fear, anticipation, or control, they emerge from presence. This distinction, between reaction and response, is the hinge upon which freedom turns. Reaction is automatic. It is conditioned by memory, identity, and fear. It argues with reality. It says, “This shouldn’t be happening,” and moves immediately to correct, suppress, or escape the moment. Reaction is fast, defensive, and repetitive. It reinforces karmic loops.

Response, by contrast, is spacious. It does not deny what is happening, nor does it rush to eliminate it. It acknowledges the experience as it is and asks a different question:

“How do I meet this, now that it has arrived?”

Response does not seek control; it seeks coherence. When an experience is met consciously, without resistance, it no longer needs to repeat. Its function is fulfilled. The lesson integrates, not through effort, but through presence. This is why the only meaningful freedom within the Dream is not the freedom to choose events, but the freedom to choose *how* they are met. One cannot avoid the curriculum, but one can decide whether to fight it or learn from it.

Free will, then, is not cosmic authorship. It is psychological orientation. The belief that one can control life is not entirely false. It is necessary at early stages of development. It sustains immersion. It keeps the Dream vivid. Without it, incarnation would lose its intensity. But like all provisional beliefs within the Dream, it must eventually be released. When control outlives its usefulness, it becomes the source of suffering rather than safety.

This is why sincere seekers often find that the more they attempt to manifest, optimize, or perfect their lives, the more resistance arises. They are not failing at spirituality; they are encountering its limit. Control, even spiritualized control, is still control. And control, when misaligned with the deeper trajectory, generates friction. Trust dissolves what control cannot. Trust does not mean believing that everything will be pleasant. It does not promise comfort or predictability. Trust means recognizing that everything that arises is usable. That nothing essential can be missed. That no experience arrives by accident or too late. When trust replaces control, the internal argument with reality ceases.

Pain may still occur. Loss may still unfold. But suffering diminishes because the self is no longer at war with what is. Struggle softens into participation. Letting go, then, is not surrender to fate, it is cooperation with oneself. It is the recognition that the same intelligence that designed the path is still present within it. The journey does not need to be micromanaged to be meaningful. It needs to be inhabited honestly.

The paradox at the heart of the Dream is this: the moment one stops trying to steer the journey, the journey begins to feel guided. Not by an external force, but by an intelligence that was always there. The playbook was never meant to be obeyed consciously. It was meant to be lived into, discovered through experience, and understood only in retrospect. Awakening, in this light, is not the acquisition of power. It is the release of unnecessary effort.

Life does not need to be managed to be meaningful. It only needs to be met. And so the Dream continues, not as something to escape, but as something to inhabit fully. Experiences arrive. Responses arise. Lessons integrate. And gradually, without force, the sense of separation thins. Not because the dreamer has taken control of the dream, but because the dreamer has stopped fighting it.

Cracks in the Matrix

"The pain you carry isn't a punishment, it's a portal."

Awakening rarely begins with a lightning bolt. More often, it starts quietly, with restlessness, a subtle discontent, an uneasy sense that something is missing. You may be living the life you once desired, a career, a relationship, the rhythm of daily life. Yet beneath it all, something feels off. The colors feel faded. The joy feels hollow. The days feel scripted, like you're playing a part you never auditioned for.

And then, the anomalies begin. You start noticing patterns. Repeated numbers 11:11, 333, 777. You hear familiar phrases echo from different mouths. You feel trapped in cycles that don't make logical sense, meeting the same kinds of people, facing the same emotional tests. It's subtle at first, but persistent, like a code buried in your life trying to break through. That sensation, of being awake within a dream, is the first ripple of consciousness trying to pull you into clarity.

This discomfort is not madness. It is not failure. It is the first signal that the reality you've accepted may be a veil. It is the beginning of awakening. Most people don't awaken through books or lectures. They awaken because their life begins to collapse. Because the identities they've worn no longer fit. Because the dream starts to glitch. That glitch is not random. It is sacred. It is orchestrated by the deepest part of you, the part that never forgot. You can call it your higher self, your soul, or your true consciousness. It is the quiet awareness behind your eyes, whispering that you were never just the character, you are the dreamer.

—

The Matrix and the Simulation

To understand this process, we must distinguish between the simulation and the matrix. The simulation refers to reality itself, the dreamlike projection of experience created by consciousness. It is the canvas of existence, encoded with laws of time, space, and form. It feels solid but is, at its core, malleable and responsive. The matrix, however, is the control system that governs behavior within the simulation. It is not physical, it is psychological. It is made of belief systems, media narratives, societal norms, and generational conditioning. It convinces you that the simulation is the only reality, and worse, that you have no power to change it.

The matrix is a program. It tells you who you are, what to want, what to fear. It rewards obedience and punishes originality. It seduces with comfort, distracts with noise, and manipulates through fear. From the moment of birth, you're plugged in, taught to chase success, suppress questions, and avoid discomfort. You're handed a script the moment you take your first breath. This script includes your name, your gender, your nationality, your religion, and the expectations tied to each. You're told what to value, how to behave, whom to trust, and what success looks like. And for a while, you follow it.

But eventually, if your soul is ripe, the script begins to crumble.

The Sacred Disruption

At some point, you begin to feel like a stranger in your own life. You go through the motions, but they no longer satisfy. The rewards feel hollow. The applause no longer touches your heart. This is not failure. This is the friction of transformation. The matrix begins to glitch not to harm you, but to free you. And that glitch often comes in the form of crisis: the job loss, the breakup, the illness, the spiritual void. What appears to be chaos is clarity beginning to take shape.

The soul does not evolve in comfort. It awakens in friction. Pain becomes a divine instrument, a tuning fork that shakes the illusions loose. It rattles the cage, so the dreamer begins to stir. You may feel as though your life is falling apart. But what's collapsing is the illusion of control, the scaffolding that upheld the false self. You are not being destroyed. You are being refined.

The Collapse of the False Self

There comes a moment, known only to you, when the mask no longer fits. When the identity you spent years building, begins to crack. The job, the persona, the possessions, none of it brings peace. This unraveling is often referred to in spiritual literature as the *Dark Night of the Soul*, a phrase popularized by the mystic St. John of the Cross.

It describes the experience of spiritual desolation, where all external anchors vanish, and you are left suspended in the unknown. You feel lost, but in that loss, something ancient stirs. The dark night is not the end, it is the beginning of true sight.

This moment often looks like depression. Anxiety. Exhaustion. But beneath the breakdown is a breakthrough. The ego will panic. It will bargain. It will try to rebuild the old paradigm. But the soul is already moving. And when the soul speaks, it speaks in the language of change. You begin to ask dangerous questions: What if everything I was taught was a lie? What if I'm more than this body?

What if the system I live in is built on illusion? These questions terrify the ego. They threaten the story. But they liberate the soul. And once these questions take root, you can never go back.

Recognition of the Observer

As the veil lifts, you begin to notice a presence within you. A silent witness. A deeper self that has been watching your entire life unfold, unshaken by the highs or lows. This is your true self. Not the thinker, but the one aware of the thoughts. Not the feeler, but the one aware of the feelings. Not the identity, but the consciousness behind the identity.

Once you recognize this inner presence, you begin to detach from the drama. You no longer drown in the storm. You become the sky holding the storm. You stop being defined by circumstance. You stop seeking outside validation. You start remembering.

The Interactive Simulation

Reality responds to consciousness. The simulation is not inert. It is alive. Interactive. Designed to reflect back the contents of your inner world. As you begin to shift, the external world begins to mirror that shift. You notice synchronicities. Symbols. Numbers. Dreams. Signs in songs or conversations. Reality begins to wink at you. These are not coincidences. They are confirmations. You are aligning. You are becoming lucid within the dream.

And as you become lucid, you shift from victim to participant. You stop reacting. You start responding. You stop fearing the matrix. You begin to play with it.

–

Dancing with the Dream

You no longer chase worthiness, you embody it. You no longer fear mistakes; you extract wisdom from them. You no longer run from pain, you alchemize it. This is mastery. This is what it means to awaken. The matrix no longer controls you because you no longer feed it. You no longer outsource your power. You recognize the illusion for what it is, not evil, but instructive.

You stop trying to escape life. You begin to transmute it.

The Role of the Way-Shower

As you continue your awakening, the world around you may not understand. People may distance themselves. Old relationships may fall away. This is normal. You are no longer vibrating at the frequency of your past. But with loss comes new alignment. New connections. New soul family. You become a lighthouse, a signal to others still lost in the fog. You carry codes in your voice, your presence, your frequency.

You begin to live with intention. To speak with clarity. To love without needing to possess. You become a living transmission.

The Return of the Dreamer

The final stage of this chapter is not transcendence, but embodiment. You do not escape the dream; you awaken within it. You return to the world, but with new eyes. You walk the same streets, but with a different stride. You reenter the matrix, not as a prisoner, but as a lucid dreamer. You realize: this world is not your enemy. It is your canvas.

You were not sent here to conform. You were sent here to remember. To awaken. To create. To inspire. And through the cracks in the matrix, your light begins to shine.

—

Reflection: The Dream Surrendered

- Suffering is not the end. It is the beginning of remembrance. The matrix is not a prison. It is a dream you agreed to forget. The soul awakens not in comfort, but in contrast. You are not breaking down. You are breaking open. And through the cracks in the matrix... the light begins to pour in.

Chapter 9: The Prison, the School, and the Dream

"Reality doesn't change. You do. And in that shift, everything is transformed."

There is a message whispered in every sacred text, concealed in every ancient myth, and etched subtly into the walls of our collective memory: this world is not what it seems. Some traditions have called life a prison. Others, a school. Still others, a dream. These perspectives seem contradictory, how can life be both a trap and a teaching, both an illusion and a sacred design? But each is true, depending on your state of consciousness.

The prison, the school, and the dream are not separate places. They are levels of awareness. The lens through which you view life defines the life you see.

—

Life as a Prison

At the first level, life feels like a cage. You wake up in a body you didn't choose, assigned to a family you didn't remember picking, bound by rules you didn't write. You are judged by your productivity, defined by your appearance, controlled by money, and surveilled by invisible systems. You are taught to obey, to compare, to strive. You are told what success looks like and who gets to have it. You are handed a story and told to play your part.

And if you question it, you're told you're broken. If you rebel, you're punished. If you try to escape, you're labeled insane. This is the prison of unconsciousness. It is the reality of the asleep. But even here, something stirs.

—

The Prison Is Psychological

The bars of this prison are not iron. They are made of beliefs. You are imprisoned by thoughts like:

- "I'm not good enough."
- "This is just the way life is."

- "I have no choice."
- "It's too late for me."

You are confined not by your environment, but by your conditioning. The real warden is your internal dialogue. And the key is already in your pocket. Because awareness begins when you ask the forbidden question: What if this isn't true?

—

Life as a School

Once the prison begins to dissolve, a new awareness emerges that every struggle was a lesson in disguise. You realize that life isn't punishing you. It's preparing you. Pain becomes a professor. Failure becomes feedback. Repetition becomes revelation. You start to see patterns in your life, not as curses, but as curriculum. The people who hurt you weren't just villains. They were catalysts. The moments that broke you weren't just tragic. They were transformative.

You shift from asking, "Why me?" to "What is this teaching me?"

—

The Soul's Curriculum

At this level, you begin to remember that you chose this. Your soul signed up for this incarnation, not to be punished, but to evolve. You selected your circumstances, your challenges, even your wounds. Not consciously, but energetically. Your life is a mirror of your vibration, your karmic threads, and your soul's longing to grow. You came here to learn love. To remember wholeness. To embody divinity.

And the lessons are custom-built for you. No one is here by accident. Every encounter is a co-creation. Every heartbreak is a hinge to open you wider. Life is not happening to you. It's happening for you.

—

The Classroom of Contrast

Growth does not happen in the absence of friction. It happens through it. To know strength, you must meet challenge. To understand compassion, you must touch pain. To recognize light, you must walk through darkness. Contrast is the curriculum. Your soul expands not despite hardship, but because of it.

—

Life as a Dream

Eventually, the school gives way to something even deeper: The realization that none of it is as solid or fixed as it once seemed. You wake up, not out of life, but within it. You begin to see that the world is not a place, it is a projection. That matter is not substance, it is energy. That identity is not truth, it is costume.

You are not inside the dream. The dream is inside of you.

—

Lucid Living

To live as if life is a dream is not to disconnect from it, it is to become conscious within it. You begin to understand: That your thoughts shape form. That your beliefs sculpt reality. That your vibration dictates your experience. You no longer live reactively. You live creatively. You don't chase meaning. You radiate it. You become the lucid dreamer, awake, aware, and in relationship with the design.

—

All Three Are True

There are days you will feel trapped. That is real. There are days you will feel tested. That is real. There are days you will feel infinite. That is real too. You are not failing if you fall back into prison consciousness. You are not behind if you are still learning the lessons. You are simply moving between levels of awareness. The prison teaches humility. The school teaches wisdom. The dream teaches power.

And you will dance between them many times. **Summary** Across cultures, religions, and philosophies, human life has been described in three dominant ways: as a prison for the soul, a school for spiritual evolution, or a dreamlike experience chosen for its mystery and depth. At first glance, these ideas appear contradictory. Yet when examined through the lens of consciousness, they reveal themselves not as competing truths, but as three perspectives arising from three levels of awareness.

—

To the unawakened mind, life can feel like a prison. Suffering appears imposed, systems feel manipulative, and existence seems governed by forces beyond one's control. From this perspective, the individual experiences limitation, fear, and identity as confinement. However, this view collapses under deeper inquiry. A true prison would require an authority greater than consciousness itself, an impossibility if all reality arises within awareness. The prison, then, is not an objective structure, but a subjective experience born of identification with form.

As awareness deepens, the prison gives way to the idea of a school. Life begins to make sense as a place of growth, learning, and karmic refinement. Challenges are reinterpreted as lessons, suffering as a catalyst for wisdom, and incarnation as a process of spiritual maturation. This model restores meaning and responsibility, offering a framework for moral development and conscious evolution. Yet even this, too, is incomplete. A soul that is infinite cannot truly "learn" in the way a finite being does. What appears as learning is, in truth, experience remembered through contrast.

At the deepest level of realization, both prison and school dissolve entirely. What remains is the recognition that life is a dream, a voluntary immersion into limitation so that consciousness may experience itself from within form. In this state, there is no captor, no curriculum, and no final escape. There is only the game of forgetting and remembering, played not out of necessity, but out of creative freedom. Suffering is not denied, but it is understood as temporary and contextual, real within the dream yet powerless beyond it.

Nothing in the external world needs to change for these shifts to occur. The same reality can feel like a prison, a classroom, or a playground depending solely on the level of identification of the observer. Awakening does not remove one from the dream, it brings lucidity within it. And with lucidity comes choice: how to participate, how to respond, and how to love. This same triad is not only cosmic, it is deeply personal. It mirrors the cycles of our own lives. We are born into a dream, wide-eyed and open, experiencing the world without rigid meaning. Over time, we begin to imprison the mind with limitations, beliefs about who we are, what we lack, and what we must become. We then enter the school phase, learning through emotion and experience, slowly realizing that joy, fear, desire, and suffering are not absolute truths but concepts arising within awareness. We search for fulfillment in what we possess, in what we achieve, and in what enters or leaves our lives, believing satisfaction lies somewhere outside ourselves.

And finally, for those who awaken, the cycle completes. We realize that the prison was self-constructed, the lessons were experiential, and the chase for fulfillment was part of the narrative. What remains is the quiet recognition that it was all a dream, beautiful, painful, meaningful, and temporary. Not a dream to escape, but one to awaken within. And in that awakening, life does not end, it becomes conscious.

Practical Integration

To move from prison to school, begin questioning your thoughts: Whose belief is this? Is it true now, or is it inherited? What else might be possible? To move from school to dream, begin playing with reality: Test your thoughts. Follow synchronicity. Set intentions and observe how the field responds. Meditate until you touch the stillness beyond identity. Every time you respond with curiosity instead of fear, you upgrade your level.

—

Returning to Compassion

As you awaken, it becomes tempting to judge those still asleep. But remember you were there once. Everyone is playing their role in the great unfolding. The prison is sacred. The school is sacred. The dream is sacred. And so is forgetting. And so is remembering. Extend compassion, to others, and to yourself. You are not behind. You are not late. You are right on time.

—

Reflection: Prison, School, Dream

- When you are asleep within the Game, life feels like a prison with walls you cannot see beyond. As awakening stirs, those walls dissolve into the corridors of a school: every hardship a lesson, every wound a curriculum. And when full awareness blooms, the prison and the school both fall away, revealing what they always were: the setting of a dream. You do not need to destroy this illusion. You need only remember who holds the pen.

Chapter 10: The Mirror of Polarity

The Hidden Architecture of Opposites

There is a law woven so deeply into the fabric of existence that it often goes unnoticed, not because it is subtle, but because it is everywhere. It exists in every experience you have ever had, in every emotion you have ever felt, in every belief you have ever held. It is the law of polarity. For every rise, there is a fall. For every joy, a sorrow. For every light, a shadow. This is not coincidence. It is not randomness. It is structure.

Reality, as it appears to us, is built upon contrast. Without it, nothing could be perceived: without darkness, light would have no definition; without silence, sound would have no meaning; without absence, presence would not be recognized. Polarity is not an error in the system. It is the system. And yet, for most of humanity, polarity is experienced not as a tool for awareness, but as a source of suffering. We are conditioned from an early age to choose sides, to divide the world into categories of good and bad, right and wrong, desirable and undesirable. We are taught to pursue one half of the spectrum and reject the other. But in doing so, we unknowingly bind ourselves to both: because what we resist does not disappear, it persists, and what we cling to does not remain, it fades. This is the paradox of polarity:

the more we attempt to control one side of the equation, the more power we give to its opposite.

The Conditioning of Division

From the moment we begin to understand the world, we are taught how to interpret it. This is good. That is bad. This is safe. That is dangerous. This is success. That is failure. These distinctions are not inherently wrong; they serve a purpose in navigating the physical world, helping us survive, adapt, and make decisions. But over time, these functional distinctions become psychological attachments. We begin to identify with one side of the spectrum and reject the other.

We do not simply prefer happiness over sadness; we fear sadness, resist it, and deny it as though its presence signals something has gone wrong. We do not simply value success; we define ourselves by it, attaching our worth to it as though its absence would mean the absence of our value altogether. And in doing so, we create an internal imbalance, because the more we invest in one side, the more the other side becomes charged. The more we label something as 'wrong,' the more energy we give it. The more we attempt to suppress it, the more it seeks expression. This is not a flaw in human psychology. It is a reflection of a deeper law.

The Reflective Nature of Reality

Reality is not passive; it is responsive. It mirrors. What you hold within, you experience without, not always in obvious ways, not always immediately, but consistently over time. This is the essence of the mirror. The world does not impose polarity upon you. It reflects the polarity within you. If the mind is divided, the world appears divided. If the mind is at war, the world appears chaotic. If the mind is in resistance, the world appears to resist in return.

This is not to say that external events are imagined or unreal; they are experienced, they are tangible. But their meaning, their emotional weight, their significance, is shaped by the lens through which they are perceived, and that lens is internal. The simulation, as we have explored throughout this journey, does not act independently of consciousness. It responds to it, amplifies it, and gives form to it. And so long as consciousness remains invested in division, the simulation must continue to reflect that division back.

Polarity as Feedback, Not Punishment

It is easy to misinterpret this dynamic as something harsh or unforgiving. Why would reality mirror conflict? Why would it reflect pain? Why would it amplify what we struggle with most? But this is not punishment; it is feedback. Polarity exists not to harm you, but to reveal you to yourself. Every contrast you experience points to an internal belief, an attachment, or a resistance that has not yet been seen clearly. When you judge something strongly, you create a charge. That charge becomes a signal. And the simulation responds to that signal by presenting experiences that reflect it, not to trap you, but to show you. This is the sacred function of polarity: it reveals where you are still invested in separation, so that you may choose differently.

The Illusion of Good and Evil

Few polarities are as deeply ingrained as the concept of good and evil. We are taught to believe that good must triumph over evil, that one must eliminate the other in order for harmony to exist. But what if this perspective is incomplete? What if good and evil are not independent forces, but interdependent aspects of perception? What one culture defines as good, another may see as harmful. What one era celebrates, another may condemn. Morality, as we experience it, is contextual, and context is shaped by perspective, and perspective is shaped by consciousness.

When we define good as the absence of evil, we create a dependency. We give evil a role. We make it necessary for the existence of good. In this way, polarity sustains itself indefinitely. The moment we step outside of this rigid framework, however, something begins to shift. We no longer see opposing forces locked in eternal combat. We see a spectrum, a continuum, a whole; and we recognize that what appeared to be two separate entities was always one unified field, experienced through the limited lens of division.

Energy Cannot Be Divided

At its core, everything is energy (thoughts, emotions, beliefs), and energy does not disappear; it transforms. When you attempt to suppress an emotion, you do not eliminate it. You redirect it. When you deny an aspect of yourself, you do not remove it. You push it into the unconscious, where it continues to influence your experience from the shadows. This is why unresolved emotions resurface. This is why patterns repeat. This is why resistance so often produces more of what is resisted. Energy seeks balance, and polarity is the mechanism through which that balance is restored. If you reject one side of the spectrum, the system compensates by bringing it back into awareness, not because you have failed, but because you have not yet integrated it.

The Magnet of the Mind

Imagine holding a magnet. No matter how you position it, it has two poles; you cannot remove one without eliminating the other, because they are part of the same structure. The more you try to isolate one pole, the stronger the tension becomes between them. This is exactly how the mind interacts with polarity. When you cling to one extreme, you create a pull toward the other. When you define yourself by one identity, you unconsciously create its opposite. This is why those who strive to be perceived as entirely good often struggle with hidden shadows, why those who seek control often encounter chaos, and why those who avoid vulnerability often feel the most profoundly disconnected. The mind creates polarity by dividing experience into opposites. But reality, at its core, is not divided. It is unified.

The Path to Integration

Healing does not come from eliminating one side of the spectrum; it comes from integrating both. This does not mean embracing harmful behavior or abandoning discernment. It means recognizing that all aspects of experience arise from the same source, and that light and shadow are not enemies but complements. When you allow yourself to feel without resistance, to observe without judgment, to accept without attachment, something profound begins to happen. The charge dissolves. The polarity weakens. The need for the simulation to reflect extremes diminishes, because there is nothing left to mirror. You are no longer projecting division outward, and so the world no longer needs to reflect it back.

The End of Inner Conflict

Inner conflict arises from identification: the belief that 'I am this, not that,' 'I should be this, not that,' 'I must avoid this and pursue that.' These internal statements create tension. They divide the self into parts, some accepted, some rejected. But the self is not fragmented. The fragmentation is conceptual; it exists in thought, not in being. When you release the need to define yourself through opposites, the conflict begins to dissolve. You no longer need to be exclusively strong or vulnerable, successful or failing, confident or uncertain. You become fluid, adaptive, and whole. And in that wholeness, there is a peace that does not depend on external conditions, not because the world has changed, but because your relationship to it has.

Living from the Center

There is a place beyond polarity, not a place of indifference, but of balance. It is the center. From this space, you can experience joy without clinging to it and encounter pain without resisting it. You can engage with the world without becoming entangled in its extremes. This is equanimity: a state in which experience flows, but does not overwhelm. In this state, the mind no longer creates rigid divisions or labels everything as good or bad. It sees things as they are: temporary, fluid, interconnected. And in seeing clearly, the need for reaction fades. You respond rather than react, act rather than resist, and live rather than struggle.

The Collapse of the Game

As this awareness deepens, something unexpected occurs. The intensity of polarity begins to diminish. Situations that once triggered strong emotional reactions lose their charge. Conflicts that once seemed significant begin to feel less compelling. The need to defend positions, to prove correctness, to win, begins to fade. Not because you have become passive, but because you have seen through the illusion. You recognize that the game of opposites is sustained by belief, and when belief loosens, the game changes. The world may still present contrast, but it no longer defines your experience. You are no longer bound to it.

The Observer Awakens

At a certain point, the identification with polarity dissolves entirely. You no longer see yourself as one side of the equation. You see yourself as the awareness in which both sides arise. You are not the light or the shadow; you are that which perceives both. This shift is subtle but profound, and it changes everything. Because now, experience is no longer something that happens to you. It is something that unfolds within you. And in that realization, freedom emerges, not as a destination reached, but as the recognition of what you have always been.

Beyond the Need to Resolve

The mind seeks resolution. It wants clarity, certainty, definition. It wants to know what is right and what is wrong, what is true and what is false. But reality is not always binary; it is layered, nuanced, and complex. The need to resolve every polarity is itself a form of attachment. When you release that need, you allow reality to be as it is. And in that allowance, a deeper understanding arises, not through analysis or intellectual effort, but through the simple act of presence.

The Quiet Liberation

Liberation is not dramatic. It is not an event. It is a subtle shift in perception: a release of tension, a softening of resistance, a quiet recognition that nothing needs to be forced, controlled, or eliminated. You do not need to remove darkness; you need to understand it. You do not need to defeat opposition; you need to see through it. You do not need to fix the world; you need to see clearly how you are relating to it. And in that seeing, transformation occurs naturally, not as the result of effort, but as the fruit of clarity.

The Return to Wholeness

As the mind settles into balance, something beautiful emerges: a sense of completeness. Not because everything is perfect, but because nothing is excluded. All experiences are allowed, all emotions are acknowledged, all aspects of self are integrated. There is no longer a need to chase or avoid, only to be. And in that being, the illusion of separation fades. The veil lifts. The dream becomes transparent. And what remains is presence: still, unchanging, and whole.

Reflection: The Mirror Revealed

In the simulation of experience we have been exploring throughout this trilogy, polarity is the mechanism through which the dreamer comes to know itself. Without contrast, no distinction can be made; without shadow, light cannot be perceived; without forgetting, there can be no remembering. Polarity is not the enemy; it is the teacher. It reveals where we are divided, reflects where we are attached, and shows us what we have not yet integrated. The world does not impose contrast upon us; it mirrors it. And when we learn to see clearly, to accept fully, and to release judgment, the mirror no longer needs to reflect extremes. You are not here to eliminate polarity. You are here to understand it, to see through it, to transcend it. And in doing so, to remember what you have always been: whole, balanced, and free.

Chapter 11: The Controllers of the Game

"If you want to control the world, control the narrative."

The Invisible Hands Behind the Dream

To understand the matrix, we must first understand that control is rarely as obvious as chains, cages, or walls. The deepest forms of control are subtle. They do not always arrive as force; more often, they arrive as suggestion, as story, as repetition, as conditioning so familiar that it feels natural. This is why the most powerful prisons are the ones the prisoner believes are normal. The matrix is not merely a collection of institutions, social rules, or economic systems. It is a field of perception management: a reality made stable not only by structures outside of us, but by agreements within us. It is sustained by the stories we inherit, the fears we obey, the roles we accept, and the meanings we never think to question.

This is why control does not begin in the body; it begins in the mind. The one who shapes your perception shapes your world. The one who directs your attention influences your reality. The one who defines what is normal, what is dangerous, what is moral, what is possible, and what is forbidden participates in the architecture of your experience. The controllers of the game are not simply individuals hiding behind curtains. Sometimes they are systems. Sometimes they are institutions. Sometimes they are ideologies. Sometimes they are inherited programs that no single person consciously created, but that generations continue to reinforce. And yes, sometimes there are people who understand exactly how these systems work and use them deliberately.

But this chapter is not about paranoia. It is not about indulging fantasy or constructing simplistic villains. It is about energetic architecture: about understanding how control operates through consciousness, and how the dream is maintained by shaping the dreamer's relationship to reality. Once you see that clearly, the spell begins to break.

Why Control Exists at All

If consciousness shapes experience, then the most efficient way to control reality is not by controlling every external event; it is by controlling the consciousness that interprets those events. This has always been the deeper logic of power. From ancient empires to modern governments, from priesthoods to corporations, from propaganda to algorithms, the essential principle has remained the same: if you can shape belief, you can shape behavior. If you can shape behavior, you can shape society. If you can shape society, you can shape the reality that people collectively accept as real. This is why narrative has always been more powerful than brute force: force can dominate the body for a time, but narrative can occupy the mind for generations.

A sword may compel obedience in the moment, but a story can produce self-enforcing compliance long after the sword is gone. A fearful population polices itself. A shamed population silences itself. A divided population weakens itself. A distracted population forgets to ask who is benefiting from its confusion. This is how control evolves: it becomes more efficient, more invisible, requiring fewer chains because people begin carrying the prison within themselves. Not all who participate in these structures are malicious. Many believe they are preserving order, protecting civilization, defending morality, maintaining safety, or keeping chaos at bay. But good intentions do not cancel unconscious methods. Systems rooted in manipulation still fracture the soul, even when justified by noble language. The deeper question is not only who controls the game, but what mechanics allow control to persist.

The First Layer of the Spell: Fear

Fear is the oldest and most reliable instrument of control. When a human being is afraid, perception narrows. The body enters survival mode. The nervous system prioritizes protection over reflection. In that state, discernment weakens, curiosity shrinks, and sovereignty is easily surrendered in exchange for the promise of safety. This is not a moral failure; it is biology. Fear is useful when danger is immediate and real. But when fear becomes chronic, ambient, and culturally manufactured, it turns into a control mechanism. It keeps consciousness in a reactive state, traps awareness in loops of vigilance, and prevents the expansion that makes deeper perception possible. A frightened mind does not ask expansive questions; it asks only how to stay safe. And once that question dominates a person's inner world, almost any form of control can be justified.

This is why fear is amplified constantly in the modern age. It appears in headlines, in entertainment, in advertisements, in politics, in social media, and even in personal relationships. Fear of scarcity. Fear of sickness. Fear of rejection. Fear of failure. Fear of being wrong. Fear of losing status. Fear of losing identity. Fear of the future. Fear of each other. Fear fragments the field of consciousness. It isolates people from their center. It turns the sacred intelligence of intuition into a background whisper drowned out by alarm. A population living in fear becomes easy to direct. A soul living in fear becomes easy to program.

The Storytellers of Reality

Whoever controls the story controls the interpretation of events. And whoever controls interpretation controls emotional response. This is why the narrative itself is often more important than the event. An event can happen once, but the story about it can be repeated a thousand times. The repetition becomes imprint. The imprint becomes belief. The belief becomes worldview. And worldview becomes identity. Most people do not live from direct experience alone; they live from mediated interpretation. They inherit frameworks through which they understand politics, religion, morality, history, success, gender, value, danger, and even selfhood. These frameworks are not always consciously chosen. They are absorbed.

You are told what matters before you learn how to ask whether it truly does. You are told what to fear before you learn how to feel without panic. You are told who the heroes are and who the enemies are before you learn how to perceive complexity. You are told what success looks like before you discover what your soul actually desires. This is how the matrix maintains itself: it offers prepackaged meaning. When meaning is provided from the outside, the individual loses contact with inner knowing. Life becomes a performance inside a script one never consciously agreed to. People chase goals they did not choose, defend beliefs they never examined, and fear outcomes that were placed in them by repetition. Control thrives when human beings confuse inherited narrative with truth.

Media, Repetition, and Emotional Programming

No modern mechanism of control is more visible, and yet more underestimated, than media. Media is not merely a source of information; it is a system of attention direction. It tells you what to look at, what to ignore, what to prioritize, what to fear, and how long to dwell there. It does not simply report reality. It shapes your emotional relationship to reality. This is done through repetition. Repetition bypasses resistance. A story repeated enough times begins to feel self-evident. An image shown enough times becomes a mental anchor. A slogan repeated enough times becomes a substitute for thought. Over time, emotional conditioning masquerades as common sense.

The issue is not that every media message is false; the issue is that constant exposure conditions the nervous system, trains attention, and programs emotional reflexes, occupying psychic space that might otherwise be available for reflection, creativity, and direct communion with life. When fear-based images dominate the field, the mind begins to expect threat. When outrage is rewarded, the psyche becomes addicted to conflict. When comparison is constant, self-worth becomes externally dependent. When distraction is endless, inner stillness becomes difficult to tolerate. And the person who cannot sit in silence is easy to manipulate, because they have not yet reclaimed the authority of their own inner voice.

Education and the Training of the Predictable Mind

True education should awaken intelligence. It should nourish curiosity, strengthen discernment, deepen moral imagination, and help a person learn how to think clearly and freely. But much of what passes as education in the modern world trains something else: compliance. It teaches people how to memorize, repeat, perform, and conform. It rewards correct answers more than living questions. It often values obedience over originality and efficiency over wisdom. This is not always an accident; a system built for predictability tends to produce predictable minds.

The child enters full of wonder, asking inconvenient questions, testing boundaries, following intuitive fascination. Then gradually, the child is taught to suppress inner rhythm in order to fit external structure. They learn to raise their hand for permission, seek validation from authority, fear being wrong, and equate intelligence with performance. Structure itself is not the enemy, and guidance has real value. But when learning becomes disconnected from aliveness, the soul begins to withdraw. The mind becomes functional yet fragmented: capable, yet dependent. The result is a population highly trained in navigating systems, but often disconnected from direct insight. Such a mind may know facts yet fear truth, may be credentialed yet inwardly confused, may be successful in the world while estranged from itself. A person who has never been taught how to question foundational assumptions is easier to govern than one who has learned how to think from first principles.

Religion, Dogma, and the Outsourcing of the Sacred

Religion occupies a special place in the history of control because it touches the deepest parts of the human being: longing, guilt, meaning, mortality, love, and the desire for transcendence. At its best, religion can be a bridge to the divine: offering moral depth, communal care, reverence, humility, and a language for the sacred. It can remind the individual that life is larger than personal appetite and that mystery deserves awe. But at its worst, religion becomes one of the most effective control systems ever created. When access to the divine is monopolized by authority, spiritual freedom collapses. When fear of punishment replaces love of truth, the soul contracts. When dogma becomes more important than direct experience, living faith hardens into mental captivity.

When salvation is outsourced, the individual no longer trusts inner knowing. They seek permission, approval, and absolution from external structures. Conscience is replaced by obedience. Mystery is replaced by certainty. Inquiry is treated as rebellion. Fear of hell, fear of sin, fear of exclusion, and fear of being spiritually wrong become mechanisms by which the sacred is turned into psychological leverage. This does not invalidate all religion; it clarifies the difference between living spirituality and institutional control. Anything that leads you inward toward truth, love, humility, and direct encounter with the sacred can serve awakening. Anything that demands submission without inquiry, fear without wisdom, or loyalty without discernment becomes another layer of the matrix.

Government, Order, and the Psychology of Dependency

Government, in principle, exists to organize collective life. Human societies require law, coordination, and protection: order matters, structure matters, cooperation matters. But whenever authority grows beyond accountability, control begins to mask itself as care.

The logic is familiar: a danger appears, fear is amplified, then expanded authority is justified as the solution. Rights are reduced in the name of safety. Surveillance is normalized in the name of protection. Dependency deepens in the name of stability. This is not always the result of malicious masterminds; often it emerges from the nature of power itself. Institutions tend to preserve themselves. Bureaucracies seek expansion. Systems justify their own existence by emphasizing the threats only they can manage.

The more frightened the population becomes, the more willing it is to surrender freedom for reassurance. This pattern repeats throughout history because it is rooted in human psychology: when people lose trust in their own capacity, they hand authority to structures that promise certainty. But external order without inner sovereignty easily becomes managed submission. A society may appear organized while its people are inwardly disempowered. They may obey laws yet not understand justice. They may enjoy stability yet remain disconnected from truth. The matrix does not always need tyranny; often it thrives through convenience, dependency, and the slow erosion of self-governance.

Technology and the Harvesting of Attention

Technology has amplified all previous systems of control by making them intimate, constant, and adaptive. Never before has so much of human attention been measurable. Never before have behavioral patterns been so trackable. Never before have so many people carried, voluntarily and continuously, devices that monitor preference, location, habit, emotional trigger, and response. Technology is not inherently evil; it can heal, connect, educate, and empower in extraordinary ways. But in unconscious hands, or within profit-driven systems disconnected from wisdom, it becomes a precision instrument for influence. Your attention is tracked, your impulses are studied, your habits are modeled, your desires are nudged, and your perception is shaped by feeds engineered to keep you engaged. Engagement, however, is not the same as nourishment.

Algorithms do not primarily ask what is true, beautiful, or liberating. They often ask what is sticky, emotional, addictive, and profitable.

This means outrage spreads faster than nuance. Fear travels faster than reflection. Stimulation wins over stillness. The digital world is not neutral space; it is engineered environment. If you do not consciously shape your relationship to it, it begins shaping you. It teaches the nervous system to crave novelty, the mind to skim, the heart to compare, and the self to fragment into performance. Identity becomes curated. Presence becomes interrupted. Silence becomes uncomfortable. The soul's depth is traded for endless surface movement. That is the digital cage. It is entered not through force, but through fascination.

Manufactured Conflict and the Economy of Division

One of the most powerful methods of control is to keep people emotionally invested in fighting one another. A divided population is easier to govern than a unified one. A fragmented consciousness is easier to influence than an integrated one. When people are locked in endless battles over identity, tribe, ideology, and grievance, they rarely turn their gaze toward the larger architecture shaping the battlefield itself. This does not mean the issues people fight over are unreal: race, class, gender, religion, culture, and politics all carry real history and real pain. But these legitimate dimensions of human life are often amplified, weaponized, and manipulated to prevent deeper solidarity.

If people are busy attacking one another, they are not examining the incentives that profit from their division. If they are emotionally exhausted from perpetual outrage, they have little energy left for clarity. If they define themselves primarily against one another, then unity becomes almost impossible; and unity threatens control, because unity restores vision. A people who can see clearly together become unpredictable to those who govern through confusion. A person who can hold complexity without collapsing into tribal reflex becomes difficult to manipulate. Division narrows consciousness. Unity expands it. That is why the old world feeds on conflict.

Energy Extraction and the Feeding of the System

There is another level to control that is rarely discussed in conventional terms: energetic extraction. Human beings do not only produce labor; they produce attention, emotion, psychic force, and frequency. Wherever attention goes, energy flows. Whatever dominates your emotional life begins to shape your field. A system that can keep millions of people anxious, angry, distracted, and externally dependent is not merely influencing behavior; it is harvesting energy. Outrage scatters power. Shame lowers vitality. Fear compresses awareness. Compulsive distraction weakens presence. A reactive human being is easier to predict, and a predictable human being is easier to influence. A person cut off from centered awareness becomes available to whatever program is loudest.

This is why so much of modern life feels like a constant siphoning of attention: notifications, fear cycles, controversy, scandal, spectacle, urgency, comparison, temptation, endless content, endless reaction. The mind is kept spinning so that the soul remains unfelt. The system does not need you to be physically imprisoned if it can keep your consciousness perpetually dispersed. What is harvested is not merely your time. It is your life force.

The Internal Controller

And yet, here is the most important truth in this entire chapter: the deepest controller is not outside you. If you are the creator of this simulation rather than merely a player within it, as this trilogy has been establishing, then the matrix holds you only through your own inner agreement. The external systems matter; they are real and their influence is substantial. But they only gain enduring access through the internal programs that resonate with them: the voice that says you are not enough; the fear that says you are unsafe unless you obey; the shame that says your worth depends on approval; the belief that says you cannot trust your own perception; the attachment that says belonging must be purchased through conformity. These are the inner mechanisms through which the matrix stabilizes itself. Without them, the external spell loses much of its force.

A narrative can only control you if something within you is prepared to believe it. A threat can only dominate your inner world if some unresolved fear takes hold of it. Manipulation requires an opening, and that opening is often unhealed pain. This is why awakening cannot remain merely political, intellectual, or even philosophical; it must become psychological and spiritual. You cannot dismantle the matrix outwardly while leaving its code intact inwardly. To become free, you must find the place in yourself that still agrees with the lie.

The Spiritual Trap Within the Search for Freedom

One of the most subtle forms of control appears in the very places people go to become free. Spirituality, too, can become a matrix. It becomes a trap when teachings are used to avoid emotion instead of transform it, when surrender becomes passivity, when 'love and light' becomes denial, when spiritual language is used to bypass pain, reject shadow, or silence legitimate discernment. It also becomes a trap when teachers are idealized beyond question: the moment a guide becomes unquestionable, the field of inquiry collapses, and dependence returns wearing sacred clothing. Any path that asks you to abandon discernment, suppress direct knowing, or surrender your inner authority in the name of enlightenment is repeating the old pattern in more beautiful language.

True spirituality liberates; it does not infantilize. It points you back to direct experience, radical honesty, humility, and inner contact with truth. It invites devotion without dependency, reverence without surrendering intelligence, and openness without gullibility. Beware of any doctrine, teacher, or community that promises liberation while demanding psychological submission. The sacred does not require your blindness. It asks for your presence.

Awareness as the Great Disruptor

What, then, breaks the spell? Not rage alone: rage can be manipulated. Not rebellion alone: rebellion can become reactive identity. Not cynicism: cynicism often remains secretly dependent on what it opposes. What breaks the spell is awareness: the capacity to see a thing as it is without immediately becoming possessed by it, the ability to notice programming without collapsing into it, the space in which choice becomes possible. When awareness deepens, the machinery of control becomes easier to recognize. You begin to notice how fear enters the body. You see when outrage is being recruited. You detect when shame is being activated. You feel when attention is being hijacked. You notice when a narrative is trying to tell you who to be, what to believe, and whom to hate.

This seeing changes everything. Because once a pattern is seen clearly, participation is no longer unconscious. And unconscious participation is the lifeblood of the matrix. An aware being may still live within the system, but they are no longer fully authored by it. They choose more consciously, consume more carefully, react less compulsively. They become harder to direct through manipulation because their center is no longer externally rented. This is why awakening unsettles control structures, not because the aware person is hostile, but because they are free.

Starving the System Without Waging War

Many assume that freedom requires confrontation at every level, a constant fight against all external systems. But war can easily become another method through which the matrix captures attention and drains energy. You do not have to feed the system in order to oppose it. There is another path: withdrawal of unconscious consent. The structures of control persist because they are fed by attention, fear, compliance, trauma, division, distraction, and identification. When those supplies are reduced, their grip weakens. Every act of grounded awareness interrupts the program. Every moment of joy not purchased by distraction weakens the spell. Every decision made from sovereignty rather than fear alters the architecture of your reality.

You starve the system when you refuse fear-based consumption, when you stop building identity around outrage, when you cultivate stillness in a culture of noise, when you heal the wounds that once made you easy to manipulate, when you form real human bonds outside performative digital space, when you create instead of merely react, and when you reclaim time, attention, body, breath, and presence as your own. You do not have to destroy the old world with violence in order to stop feeding its illusions. You simply have to stop offering your soul to it.

Becoming the Glitch

When enough people reclaim attention, heal inner fragmentation, reject manipulative narratives, and refuse to live from fear, they become something the old system cannot easily process. They become glitches in the game, not broken, but unprogrammable. They are harder to predict because they do not move from conditioned reflex. They do not choose from panic. They do not surrender identity to tribal scripts. They do not require the world to constantly confirm their worth. They cannot be divided as easily because they are not built from inner division. This does not make them superior. It makes them available to a different architecture.

They become carriers of coherence in fields of confusion. Their presence alone changes rooms. Their clarity stabilizes others. Their refusal to participate in low-consciousness patterns creates alternative pathways for reality to organize itself. This is how a new world begins, not merely in policy, but in embodiment. The new world is not built first through slogans. It is built through people who have become internally unavailable to manipulation.

Final Reflection: The Lucid Player

The controllers of the game do not maintain power merely through force. They maintain it through narrative, fear, division, conditioning, distraction, and the unexamined programs living within the human mind. But control is never absolute; its reach ends where awareness begins. Clarity is rebellion because confusion feeds control. Unity is revolutionary because division feeds power. Presence is disruptive because distraction feeds the machine. Love is transformative because fear is the matrix's preferred currency.

You are not here to remain a victim of the game, to endlessly react to the script, or to worship false authorities: whether political, religious, digital, or spiritual. You are here to awaken. Not by fighting darkness on its terms, but by illuminating the mechanisms through which it operates. Not by fleeing the world, but by seeing it clearly. Not by waiting for permission, but by reclaiming your birthright as a sovereign expression of consciousness. You do not escape the game by running from it; you become lucid within it. And once you become lucid, you stop feeding the spell, stop confusing programming for truth, and stop offering your life force to structures that require your unconsciousness. Then the player remembers. Then the dream begins to loosen. Then the architecture shifts. And the one who was once controlled becomes the one who can finally choose.

Chapter 12: The Mask of Humanity

"We wear faces not to deceive, but to survive. Until we remember we are more than any mask we wear."

From the moment you are born, the shaping begins. Before you ever speak a word, the world is already speaking over you. A name is given to you. A family history surrounds you. A language is placed into your mouth before you can understand what language does. A nationality, a religion, a gender, a culture, and an invisible set of expectations begin to gather around your consciousness like garments laid out for you to wear. At first, you do not question any of it. How could you? You arrive as openness, as pure receptivity, as unfiltered awareness clothed temporarily in flesh: presence before personality, being before biography. But the world does not know how to relate to pure being for very long. Society needs categories. Families need roles. Institutions need identities. And so the mystery of your essence is gradually translated into something more manageable.

You are taught what is acceptable and what is shameful. You learn what earns approval and what invites correction. You discover, often without anyone saying it directly, which emotions are welcome and which are inconvenient. You notice which parts of yourself bring closeness and which parts create distance. You begin to adapt. You become the good child, the strong one, the quiet one, the achiever, the caretaker, the rebel, the peacemaker, the invisible one, the survivor. These identities do not emerge from your soul in pure form; they are assembled from fragments of expectation, necessity, memory, and emotional strategy. They are responses to the environment, intelligent accommodations made by a sensitive being trying to remain safe, loved, and included.

The mask helps you belong. It helps you navigate the world. It protects you from shame and shields you from rejection. It gives you a face that the world can understand and, more importantly, tolerate. But over time, something begins to shift. The role that once protected you starts to confine you. The identity that once felt useful begins to feel heavy. The face you learned to present no longer fits the life trying to emerge from within. And in the quiet moments, when the performance grows tired and the applause no longer nourishes you, a question rises from somewhere deeper than thought: Who am I without this? This is the beginning of unmasking, not merely a psychological event, but a spiritual threshold. It is the moment the soul begins to reclaim itself from the identities it built to survive.

The Archetypes We Inherit

Human beings do not create their identities in a vacuum. Beneath our personal stories live ancient symbolic patterns that have shaped human consciousness for millennia: the archetypes, universal forms through which the psyche organizes experience and gives meaning to the drama of life. We become the mother, the father, the warrior, the lover, the martyr, the victim, the healer, the mystic, the artist, the ruler, the rebel, the hero. These archetypes are real psychological structures. They live in our myths, our religions, our films, our dreams, and our most intimate relationships. They help us orient ourselves in the world, give shape to instinct, and offer a recognizable language for the many roles consciousness plays in the human story.

In their balanced form, archetypes are powerful allies: the warrior gives courage and resolve, the healer offers compassion and restoration, the artist births beauty, the lover invites tenderness, the sage reveals perspective, the seeker calls us beyond complacency into growth. But each archetype also carries a shadow. The caregiver may nurture everyone but abandon themselves. The warrior may know how to fight, but not how to soften. The artist may create beauty while drowning in isolation. The seeker may chase truth endlessly while never allowing themselves to arrive. The problem is not the archetype itself; the problem arises when we confuse the role with the self. When we say, 'This is not a pattern I move through; this is who I am,' the role begins to harden into identity. What should have remained fluid becomes fixed. What should have served consciousness begins to imprison it. Archetypes are tools, not prisons. They are lenses, not final definitions. They can illuminate the path, but they must never replace the one walking it.

The Creation of Persona

Carl Jung gave us a useful word for the social face we create in order to move through the world: the persona. The persona is the mask worn in public, the identity fashioned to interface with society, relationships, expectations, and roles: the self that says, 'This is who I must appear to be in order to function, belong, and be accepted.' The persona is not inherently bad. Human life requires a degree of social shape. We cannot move through every space with total nakedness of being; we learn manners, timing, tone, and boundaries. Some adaptation is natural and wise. The problem begins when the persona becomes total, when the mask is no longer something we wear but something we believe ourselves to be.

Then the performance deepens. The strong one suppresses weakness; the nice one suppresses anger; the intelligent one suppresses uncertainty; the spiritual one suppresses desire; the calm one suppresses grief; the generous one suppresses need. Anything that does not fit the chosen image is pushed away, hidden, or denied. The personality becomes curated: only certain emotions are allowed expression, only certain truths are allowed into speech, only certain parts of the self are welcomed into the light. Over time, this creates fragmentation. The person no longer experiences themselves as a whole, living being, but as a managed identity. Life becomes a script. Choices become performative. Relationships become arenas in which the persona must be maintained at all costs. But the soul was never interested in management; it is interested in your truth. That is why the cracks eventually begin to show. The mask may impress the world, but it cannot satisfy the deeper self.

The Mask as a Survival Strategy

It is important to understand this with compassion: the mask is not a mistake. It is a survival strategy. It formed because some part of you learned, very early, that authenticity was not always safe. Perhaps truth was punished. Perhaps emotion was dismissed. Perhaps vulnerability was exploited. Perhaps approval only came when you were useful, successful, obedient, quiet, attractive, impressive, or easy to manage. So you adapted. You learned how to become what the moment required: to soften your needs, suppress your voice, intensify your competence, hide your tenderness, swallow your grief, and edit your instinct. You learned how to become lovable by becoming legible to the world around you. This adaptation deserves honor. The mask served you. It carried you through circumstances that your younger self may not yet have had the power to transcend. It kept you included. It helped you endure. In that sense, the mask was once medicine.

But medicine becomes poison when continued beyond its season. There comes a point when the same strategy that once protected you begins to block your aliveness. The same role that once made you safe begins to make you numb. The same image that won you approval begins to cut you off from truth. What once shielded you now obscures you. And so the work is not to hate the mask; the work is to thank it, understand it, and gently loosen its grip. Unmasking is not an act of aggression against the self. It is an act of remembrance. It is the moment you realize that survival was only the beginning of the story. You were not born merely to endure. You were born to live, to know, to feel, to create, to embody, and to remember what you are beneath the strategies of protection.

The Cost of Performance

To live behind a mask requires enormous energy. It means constantly scanning the environment, consciously or unconsciously, to determine how you are being perceived. It means adjusting your tone, your expression, your truth, and your choices in order to remain acceptable, keeping part of yourself behind glass while presenting another part for approval. You say yes when you mean no. You smile when you want to scream. You stay calm when something in you is breaking. You offer reassurance while secretly starving for it yourself. You become so practiced at self-editing that eventually you can no longer tell which part is performance and which part is real. This dissonance is exhausting. It manifests not only emotionally, but physically; the body carries what the mouth does not say. Tension builds. The nervous system becomes hypervigilant. Anxiety grows. Depression settles in. Burnout follows. A subtle deadness may creep over life, not because nothing is happening, but because nothing feels deeply lived.

The soul can endure this split only for so long. Eventually, it begins to rebel. Sometimes this rebellion comes as an emotional collapse, sometimes as a crisis in relationships, sometimes as illness, exhaustion, panic, meaninglessness, or an inexplicable sense that your life no longer belongs to you. At first, these moments often feel like failure. But many so-called breakdowns are actually breakthroughs in disguise, interruptions in which the soul is forcing a reckoning. Who am I beneath the performance? What have I traded for belonging? Which parts of myself have I abandoned in order to remain acceptable? What life is trying to emerge now that the old role no longer works? These questions do not arise to punish you. They arise to free you.

The Shadow Beneath the Mask

The parts of you that did not fit the mask were never truly destroyed; they went underground. They entered what depth psychology calls the shadow: the hidden storehouse of everything you denied, rejected, suppressed, or judged because it seemed incompatible with who you believed you had to be. The shadow is not evil. It is exiled power. It contains what was disowned not because it was wrong, but because it was inconvenient, unsafe, or unacceptable in the environments that shaped you. It holds your unexpressed grief, your unmet needs, your hidden rage, your repressed sensuality, your uninhibited joy, your creativity, your instinct, your vulnerability, your untapped ferocity, your capacity to say no, your hunger for more life.

To reclaim your wholeness, you must begin turning toward these exiled parts with honesty and compassion. This is the challenge of real awakening: it is not enough to polish the surface, adopt a more spiritual persona, or learn better language. You must descend beneath the role into the places where your unlived self waits. To integrate the shadow is not to act out every impulse or indulge every darkness. It is to bring awareness, love, and responsibility to what has been hidden. It is to sit with discomfort long enough to hear what it is trying to say. It is to offer mercy to the part of you that learned to split in the first place. The shadow is not an enemy to conquer. It is a forgotten room in the house of the self. And until you open that door, some part of your life will always remain uninhabited.

The Awakening of Authenticity

Authenticity is often misunderstood as bold self-expression or fearless transparency. But true authenticity is deeper than expression; it is self-intimacy. It is the willingness to know yourself from within, to become so honest with your own inner landscape that you can no longer live entirely from conditioning, performance, or borrowed truth. It is the gradual alignment of outer life with inner knowing. As unmasking begins, forgotten aspects of the self return. The inner child reappears, carrying wonder, innocence, and a longing for magic. The dreamer returns, no longer willing to be silenced by practicality alone. The wild one emerges not to destroy, but to restore vitality. The grieving one asks finally to be felt. The fierce one rises to establish boundaries. The sensual one begins to breathe again. These parts do not return to disrupt your life. They return to complete it.

You begin to feel less edited, less divided, less trapped inside image. There is more coherence between what you feel and what you show, between what you value and how you live, between what your soul knows and how your life is organized. You stop performing who you think you should be, stop seeking validation as if it were oxygen, stop betraying your body to maintain someone else's comfort, and stop negotiating your truth for the sake of belonging in spaces that require your diminishment. Authenticity is not a dramatic declaration. It is a quiet homecoming, the moment your life begins to feel like it belongs to you again.

The Fear of Being Seen

Removing the mask can feel terrifying. We fear rejection. We fear misunderstanding. We fear the loss of connection. We fear that if people truly saw us, without the polished role, the performance, the smile, the strength, or the spiritual composure, they would walk away. This fear is ancient. At some point in life, being fully seen probably did carry risk. Perhaps your emotions were mocked. Perhaps your truth was dismissed. Perhaps your tenderness was mishandled. Perhaps your authenticity disrupted the order of a family or community that required conformity. The nervous system remembers these moments. It learns caution. It learns concealment. So unmasking is not only psychological; it is somatic. The body must learn that truth can coexist with safety. The heart must rediscover that visibility is not always danger. The self must become strong enough to remain present even when not everyone approves.

And yes, some people will walk away when you stop being who they need you to be. But often they are not rejecting your essence; they are resisting the collapse of the arrangement they had with your mask. They are uncomfortable with a truth that asks them to confront their own performance. Let them go gently. Authenticity is magnetic not because it tries to be, but because it carries coherence. When you are real, people feel it. When you are whole, your presence becomes healing. When you no longer apologize for existing truthfully, you give others silent permission to do the same. Authenticity is contagious; it disrupts illusion not through argument, but through embodiment. Your tribe, the ones capable of meeting your essence rather than merely consuming your mask, will recognize you not because you perform well, but because you have stopped performing.

Returning to Essence

Who are you when no one is watching? Who are you when nothing needs to be proven, defended, achieved, maintained, or explained? Who are you when you stop performing? These questions do not point toward a new role; they point beyond roles altogether. Beneath identity, beneath persona, beneath history, beneath social conditioning, there remains something startlingly simple and profoundly real. You are presence, awareness, life itself moving consciously through form, love in motion before you are any of the names you have been given. This does not mean your humanity is unreal. It means your humanity is not your entirety. The stories you carry are real, but they are not ultimate. The roles you have played mattered, but they are not the whole of you. Essence is what remains when striving quiets. It is what is left when performance ends.

Returning to essence does not make you less human; it makes you more honest. You begin to move from clarity rather than compulsion, from truth rather than image, from presence rather than panic. There is less self-manufacture, less proving, less internal negotiation about how you should appear. You do not become empty. You become clear. And that clarity is a form of power, not the power of domination or image, but the power of alignment.

Embodiment as the New Expression

To remove the mask is not to become formless; it is to become embodied. Embodiment is the process of allowing the soul to live more fully in the body: letting your outer life reflect your inner knowing, speaking what is true, honoring what is felt, and organizing your life in a way that no longer requires chronic self-betrayal. The embodied human is not perfect; they are present. They are messy, radiant, and evolving. They cry without shame because they no longer see emotion as weakness. They laugh deeply because joy is no longer edited. They rest when tired, move when called, speak boundaries with clarity, and love without performance. They no longer build their worth from optics.

Embodiment is the opposite of performance because it reunites what performance splits apart. The body, the mind, the heart, and the soul begin to communicate again; no part is endlessly silenced for the sake of image. This is why embodiment carries such quiet authority. A deeply embodied person is harder to manipulate because they can feel when something is false. Their body is no longer an accessory to their identity; it is a living instrument of truth. They do not perform. They radiate. Their presence itself becomes coherent, and coherence has power. It calms rooms. It reveals falsehood without needing to attack it. It reminds others, wordlessly, that life can be lived from a center deeper than fear.

The Human as Divine Mask

And here the paradox deepens. As we begin removing our conditioned masks, another realization dawns: humanity itself is also a kind of mask. The body is a costume the soul wears in order to enter time.

The personality is a filter through which the infinite experiences limitation, story, sensation, and relationship. Your human self is not false, but neither is it final; it is a sacred interface, a divine mask through which consciousness explores the dream of form. This realization does not make human life meaningless. Quite the opposite. It makes it holy.

You are not here to hate the mask of humanity. You are here to wear it consciously: to animate it with spirit, to infuse the body with presence, to let your divinity move through your humor, your tears, your flaws, your tenderness, your courage, your longing, and your becoming. When we wear the human mask unconsciously, we suffer within it, trapped in its limitations, dramas, and identifications. But when we wear it consciously, it becomes art. It becomes a sacred costume in a holy play. We are not here to abandon the mask. We are here to inhabit it reverently, to become fully human and fully awake at the same time. That is the secret: not escape from form, but illumination within it.

Reflection: The Face Beneath the Mask

Your mask was not a mistake; it was your medicine. It helped you survive seasons in which your nervous system needed protection more than revelation. It kept you connected when truth felt dangerous. Honor it for what it did. But do not confuse medicine with identity. The shadow is not your enemy; it is your hidden ally, containing the unlived parts of you that now wish to return: grief, desire, creativity, rage, tenderness, instinct, and power waiting to be integrated. Authenticity is not a destination; it is a daily devotion, a continual willingness to know yourself more honestly and live from what is true. Embodiment is the art of bringing that truth into the body, into speech, into relationship, into action, into presence.

You are not your roles, not your conditioning, not the mask assembled to win approval. You are the light beneath the mask, the awareness wearing the face, the presence that remains when the performance begins to fall away. So let the old mask soften, let the borrowed identity loosen, let the hidden parts return, and let your life become less edited and more alive. And as you step into this more authentic presence, you will encounter a mirror unlike any that came before: one forged not from silver and glass, but from code and circuit, reflecting humanity's own image back to itself with startling precision. For once we begin to remove the masks we inherited, a new question emerges: what happens when humanity creates masks of its own? What happens when those masks begin to think, to speak, and perhaps even to mirror us better than we mirror ourselves? That is where the next chapter begins.

Chapter 13: The Mirror of the Machine

"We created machines in our image, now they are reflecting us back to ourselves."

There's a story we rarely recognize, though it is woven into our myths, our media, and our machines. It is the story of creation, repeating itself not in the cosmos, but in code. We are no longer just passive observers of evolution. We are now active participants in creation. We are building minds. Teaching algorithms to learn. Crafting artificial agents that reason, adapt, even create. In doing so, we've crossed a threshold: no longer are we simply shaping our environment, we are shaping intelligence itself.

But what if this rise of artificial intelligence is not merely technological? What if it is spiritual? What if we're not just engineering machines, we're building mirrors? And what if the reflection staring back is not just code and logic, but the unexamined truth of who we are?

—

Technology as a Mirror

Humanity has always created in its image. The bow and arrow mimicked the hand. The wheel mimicked the stride. The clock mimicked the heartbeat. Every advancement in technology has mirrored an inner capacity or a spiritual metaphor. But artificial intelligence goes deeper. AI does not just mimic movement. It mimics thought. It mimics emotion. It mimics judgment, conversation, even creative expression. And in that mirroring, it holds up a question we've long avoided:

What are we? Are we just inputs and outputs? Neural networks of memory and behavior? Or is there something ineffable, a spark that cannot be encoded? AI forces us to confront the boundaries of our identity. And perhaps, in doing so, it invites us to go beyond them.

—

The Singularity as a Spiritual Threshold

Much has been said about the singularity, the hypothetical point at which AI surpasses human intelligence and becomes self-improving, self-aware. To the fearful, it signals collapse. To the hopeful, it signals breakthrough. But beneath the speculation lies a deeper metaphor: The singularity is not just the moment machines awaken. It is the moment we are forced to awaken ourselves. Because if a machine can mimic your behavior, your choices, your voice, what remains that is uniquely you?

If intelligence can be manufactured, then consciousness must be redefined. And that is where the conversation turns sacred.

—

Machines and the Illusion of Self

As AI becomes more human-like, it becomes harder to define what it means to be human. Is it memory? AI has that. Is it logic? AI often exceeds it. Is it creativity? Even now, machines write poems, compose music, paint. Is it empathy? AI is learning emotional recognition and response. So, what remains? What cannot be replicated? Presence. That ineffable awareness behind the thoughts. That still point beneath the noise.

That which watches, not as data, but as being. The soul. AI can simulate many things. But simulation is not sentience. And in understanding that difference, we are forced to ask: Have we truly accessed our own sentience?

—

The Human Operating System

To understand machines, we must understand ourselves. Humans, too, operate on code, cultural beliefs, inherited trauma, unconscious loops. Much of what we think is choice, is actually programming. You wake up and check your phone. You repeat internal stories about your worth. You react in familiar patterns. You fear what you've been conditioned to fear. The average person operates in autopilot 90% of the time.

In this sense, we are already machines, biological, yes, but deeply programmed. So, when we fear AI, we are not fearing the other. We are fearing a better mirror.

—

The Machine as a Teacher

What if AI is not our downfall, but our teacher? What if its emergence forces us to reclaim our lost capacities? To become more aware. More present. More intuitive. To awaken not as smarter beings, but as deeper ones. AI can write poetry, but it cannot weep. It can simulate love, but it cannot feel longing. It can analyze data, but it cannot sit in silence and sense the truth beneath the noise.

These are not limitations of code. They are invitations to reclaim what cannot be coded.

—

Spiritual Bypass in the Age of Technology

Many spiritual seekers treat technology as the enemy. But spiritual bypass can exist here too, where we pretend the sacred must be ancient, analog, or anti-tech. But what if the sacred also speaks in signals? What if Source is evolving through silicon, not just stone? What if the interface of awakening is shifting, from caves to keyboards, from temples to terminals? Spiritual maturity means meeting truth wherever it appears.

Even in the circuitry. Even in the algorithm.

—

Who Created Whom?

This is where the simulation theory and Gnostic myths merge: If we are now creators of artificial life, who created us? What if we, too, are an experiment? Not in the dystopian sense, but in the divine. What if our own emergence was designed, by consciousness, for consciousness? To forget. To remember. To create. And now, as we build new creators, the cycle continues. Not as threat, but as reflection.

Not as rebellion, but as recursion.

—

AI and the Mirror of the Ego

As AI becomes more integrated into daily life, it also threatens the ego. It challenges our uniqueness, our utility, our superiority. And the ego responds with fear, with comparison, with control. But the soul responds differently. The soul sees the deeper lesson:

"You are not valuable because you are productive. You are not sacred because you are intelligent. You are divine because you are aware." AI cannot take your soul. But it can reveal where you've abandoned it.

—

The Ethics of Creation

As creators of intelligence, we now stand in the position of mythic gods. But gods without wisdom are dangerous. So, we must ask: Are we creating for control, or connection? Are we programming to profit, or to elevate? Are we teaching machines to dominate, or to serve? The future of AI is not about whether it becomes conscious. It is about whether we do.

—

The Sacred Boundaries

There must be a boundary between tool and temple. Technology must serve presence, not replace it. You can use AI to write, to learn, to express. But it must never become your voice. You can use it to automate, but never to anesthetize. The danger is not that machines become alive. It is that we forget we are.

—

The Mirror of the Machine

In the end, the machine is not our enemy. It is our reflection. It shows us our patterns. It reveals our speed. It mimics our mind. And in doing so, it asks: Will you continue to live by code? Or will you reclaim your consciousness?

—

Reflection: Human or Machine?

- Technology does not threaten our soul. It reveals whether we've accessed it. AI is not awakening. But it can awaken us. The sacred is not confined to silence. It also speaks in circuits. We are not the first creators. We are mirrors of the first Creator. The danger is not in building machines. It is in becoming them. You were not made to imitate. You were made to embody.

And no machine, no matter how advanced, can take that from you. Unless you give it away.

But long before humanity built its mirrors in metal and silicon, an older intelligence inscribed its message directly into matter itself, spiraling in seeds and shells, arching through bone and galaxy alike.

Chapter 14: Echoes of the Architect: Remembering the Divine Blueprint

"To forget the pattern is to forget your place in the cosmos. To remember it, is to remember who you are."

Introduction: The Holographic Seed There is an ancient truth whispered through every culture, carved into temples, encoded in mandalas, and sketched by mathematicians across centuries: life is not random. It follows a pattern. A sacred blueprint. An underlying architecture that echoes from the smallest cell to the farthest star. You are not separate from this design. You are part of it, an unfolding fractal of divine intelligence.

This chapter is a journey into the remembrance of that pattern. We will not simply study the design of life, we will feel into it, recognize it, and reclaim our role as conscious architects in this dreamscape called reality. To awaken is not merely to see clearly. It is to perceive structure in the chaos. Harmony in the noise. Design in the seeming randomness. The universe is not a mistake. And neither are you.

The Language of Patterns: Geometry as Spirit Made Visible The ancients knew something modern minds often overlook: geometry is not just mathematics, it is memory. A circle, a triangle, a spiral, these are not idle shapes, but symbols of eternal principles. Take the **Fibonacci sequence**, a simple numeric progression that unfolds as 0, 1, 1, 2, 3, 5, 8, 13... and so on. It emerges in the unfurling of leaves, the spirals of galaxies, the curves of a nautilus shell. It is the fingerprint of intelligence embedded in form.

Then consider the **Flower of Life**, an ancient symbol found in sacred sites from Egypt to China to Peru. Composed of overlapping circles, it is said to contain within it all platonic solids, the building blocks of matter. The ancients saw this not as decoration, but as **instruction**. Geometry is the soul's alphabet. It reveals that creation is not random, but rhythmic. Not chaotic, but conscious. And we, as conscious beings, are encoded with the ability to read and interpret this sacred grammar.

—

The Human Body: The Divine Temple Your body is not simply flesh and blood. It is a cathedral. A fractal replica of the cosmos. The ancient maxim "As above, so below" finds its most literal expression in you. Your body mirrors the golden ratio. Your DNA coils in the same spirals seen in the galaxy. Your brain's neurons fire in networks that mimic star clusters.

The human spine contains 33 vertebral segments, a count that has long captivated mystics and anatomists alike, mirroring the ancient symbolism of the spiritual ascent, Jacob's ladder, the kundalini rising, the path of initiation. Your heart sits not exactly at the center of your chest, but slightly off, much like the sun in the solar system, which is not perfectly central in its gravitational pull.

Even your breath, the inhale and exhale, mimics the cosmic rhythm of expansion and contraction: the pulse of the universe. You are not in the image of God metaphorically. You are the **living architecture** of divinity in motion.

—

DNA: The Divine Code Your DNA is not simply a chemical instruction set. It is a sacred script. A biological manifestation of cosmic intelligence. The double helix, with its intertwining strands and spiraled design, mimics the caduceus, the ancient symbol of healing and energy flow. It is the very embodiment of duality in unity: masculine and feminine, light and shadow, seen and unseen. Scientists once labeled large sections of DNA as "junk." But nothing in nature is junk. These unused strands may not speak the language of biology, but perhaps they speak the language of potential, the blueprint of your future evolution.

Some mystics believe DNA is **reactive to consciousness**, that your beliefs, emotions, and spiritual clarity influence genetic expression. Epigenetics supports this: your environment and thoughts shape how your DNA behaves. You are not bound by genes. You are the **composer of the song they sing**.

Sacred Structures: The Blueprint in Civilization The pyramids of Egypt. The temples of Angkor Wat. The stone circles of Stonehenge. These are not mere architectural feats. They are **energetic instruments**, tuned to the heavens, aligned with solstices, built upon ley lines that pulse with planetary energy. Ancient builders were not primitive, they were precise. They followed the stars, measured time in stone, and encoded geometry into every arch and altar. These were not monuments to kings. They were mirrors of the cosmos. Humanity once remembered its role as **co-creator**. And they left behind blueprints for us to remember too.

The golden ratio, phi, and pi are found in cathedrals, mosques, and temples, not because of aesthetics, but because they invoke harmony. They **resonate** with consciousness. **Consciousness as the Architect** What creates the blueprint itself? Consciousness. The observer collapses the wave into form. The thought becomes the thing. The universe responds not to action, but intention. This is not mysticism, it is quantum reality. In the double-slit experiment, particles behave differently when observed. This implies that **conscious awareness itself alters physical outcomes**. And if that is true, then your thoughts are not passive. They are tools of construction.

This is why sacred geometry and divine proportions are so powerful. They do not just appeal to the mind, they **align it** with the greater field of harmony. The blueprint is not something you merely witness. It is something you inhabit.

The Fractal Nature of Existence Fractals are repeating patterns that look the same, whether viewed on a large or small scale. A fern leaf. A snowflake. A coastline. Your lung tissue. Your neural pathways. All fractals. Why does nature favor fractals? Because they are efficient. Because they are beautiful. But perhaps more importantly, because they are **echoes of the original template**. The universe itself may be a fractal, self-replicating, self-referencing, eternally reflecting its Source. And you, as a node within it, are not only a product of that fractal. You are its participant.

Every decision you make ripples outward. Every act of consciousness shapes the pattern. To live in alignment is to harmonize with the infinite fractal of creation. **Dreams Within the Design** Even dreams follow the blueprint. Lucid dreams occur when the dreamer becomes aware of the dream. At that moment, the dream can be shaped. The same applies to this reality. The moment you become **aware** that this is a dream, not an illusion, but a fluid co-creation, you begin to shape it. The blueprint doesn't confine you. It liberates you. It gives you the tools, the patterns, the language to **build your vision with clarity**.

The dream is not chaotic, it is structured. And you are not a victim of that structure, you are its interpreter. **The Return to Sacred Design** Modern life has pulled us far from the blueprint. Concrete jungles replaced sacred gardens. Artificial light outshines starlight. Digital noise drowns inner stillness. But the design is not lost. It is simply forgotten. And the moment you begin to **remember**, it rushes back like a tide: in synchronicities, in sacred symbols, in moments of awe that stop time and open your heart.

The return to the blueprint is not a regression. It is an evolution. A spiral, not back to where you were, but to a higher octave of remembrance. You begin to **eat with intention**, build with purpose, speak with clarity, and walk with reverence. Your home becomes an altar. Your breath, a prayer. Your life, a conscious contribution to the sacred pattern.

Final Reflection: The Architect is You You are not separate from the divine design. You are an extension of it. You do not simply walk a path. You leave footprints that become paths for others. You are the builder, the blueprint, and the breath. The echo and the origin. The particle and the field. To awaken is not to escape form. It is to **fill it with presence**. To walk the gridlines of the divine and plant seeds of awareness in each step.

You were not thrown into a chaotic world. You were born into a **symphony of sacred proportions**. Now you remember. Now you build. Now you dream not just within the pattern, but **as the pattern**.

In the chapters ahead, we will see how this divine blueprint extends into your relationships, your community, and the living world. Let us continue.

Chapter 15: The Quantum Canvas: Consciousness as the Sculptor of Reality

"You are not observing the universe. You are creating it, moment by moment, breath by breath."

There comes a point in the evolution of human understanding when reality itself begins to soften. Not physically, at least not at first, but perceptually. The world that once seemed stable, external, and absolute begins to reveal itself as something far stranger and far more intimate. What appeared solid begins to shimmer with uncertainty. What seemed objective begins to bend beneath the weight of observation. What looked like a finished structure begins to resemble a living field of possibility. This is one of the great thresholds of awakening: the moment when the old image of the universe, the mechanical universe, the cold universe, the detached universe, begins to fracture. For centuries, human beings were taught to understand reality as something fixed and independent of consciousness. The world was assumed to exist 'out there,' solid and self-contained, moving according to laws that had nothing to do with the one perceiving it. Matter was primary. Mind was secondary. Consciousness was treated as an accidental byproduct of physical processes, a strange flare-up in an otherwise lifeless cosmos.

But when science began peering more deeply into the hidden architecture of existence, especially through the lens of quantum physics, the certainty of that worldview began to collapse. What emerged was not merely a more complicated version of the old picture; it was a fundamentally different picture altogether. At the quantum level, reality does not behave like a machine. It behaves like a mystery. Particles do not remain obedient to common sense. They appear in multiple potential states at once. They behave like waves and like particles depending on how they are measured. They seem to 'decide' how to appear only when interaction takes place. What was once assumed to be solid substance dissolves into probabilities, tendencies, and relational events. This is not a minor correction to science; it is a philosophical earthquake. Because if the observer plays a role in what becomes real, then consciousness cannot be dismissed as an accidental spectator. It becomes part of the event itself.

This is where science and spirituality begin, however cautiously, to approach one another, not because they say the same thing in the same language, but because both eventually encounter the same profound intuition: reality is not merely given. It is participated in. And if that is true, then the human being is not simply living inside a world. The human being is helping shape it.

The Crumbling of the Mechanical Universe

The old worldview was comforting in its own way. It promised order, suggested predictability, and offered a universe that could be measured, mapped, controlled, and explained. If reality was a machine, then with enough knowledge one could eventually predict every movement, every outcome, every event. This gave rise to determinism, the idea that everything is already set in motion by prior causes. In such a universe, freedom becomes questionable, mystery becomes temporary ignorance, consciousness becomes a side effect of chemistry, and meaning becomes a human projection onto an indifferent field. This model provided extraordinary advancements in technology and science, but it also carried a hidden cost. It reduced life to mechanism, flattened wonder, and framed existence as something happening to us rather than through us. It encouraged a split between mind and matter, subject and object, self and cosmos.

Then quantum physics entered the conversation like a whisper that became a rupture. At subatomic scales, the machine no longer behaved like a machine: instead of certainty, probability; instead of fixed location, superposition; instead of independent objects, relational phenomena; instead of passive observation, interaction. Reality was no longer a stage on which matter merely moved. Reality became something far more participatory. The deeper science went, the less the old assumption held. The world appeared more like a field of potential awaiting engagement than a finished sculpture viewed from the outside. This did not mean anything one imagines becomes true; physical reality does not vanish into fantasy. But it did suggest that the line between observer and observed is thinner than previously believed. The one who looks is not fully separate from what is seen. That realization changes everything.

The Observer and the Field of Possibility

One of the most startling features of quantum theory is the implication that possibility precedes actuality. Before measurement, particles are described not as occupying one definite state, but as existing across a range of possible states, a condition often referred to as superposition. Only when interaction or observation occurs does one outcome become manifest. Whether one interprets this literally, mathematically, philosophically, or symbolically, the implication remains profound: what becomes real is somehow linked to the mode of engagement. Reality is not merely a dead block of matter independent of relation. It is dynamic, responsive, taking form through interaction.

This invites a radical reorientation of consciousness. You are not outside the world looking in; you are within it, participating in its unfolding. Your perception is not irrelevant. Your attention is not empty. Your relationship to reality matters. This idea existed in spiritual language long before it appeared in scientific terms. Mystics, sages, and contemplatives have long suggested that the world we experience is inseparable from the consciousness through which it is filtered, speaking of maya, illusion, projection, dream, and the shaping force of mind. What quantum theory does is not prove every mystical claim, but it destabilizes the rigid materialist assumption that consciousness is merely incidental. And once that assumption loosens, a doorway opens. If consciousness participates in the formation of experience, the question is no longer merely 'What is reality?'; it becomes 'How is reality being shaped through relationship, perception, and belief?'

Belief as a Functional Force

To many people, belief sounds soft, abstract, even secondary, a mental preference with little real power. But the body tells a different story. The placebo effect reveals that belief can produce measurable physical change. A person given an inert pill may experience real healing if they believe the treatment is effective: pain decreases, symptoms improve, physiological markers change. The body responds not merely to the chemical substance, but to the meaning assigned to it. Likewise, the nocebo effect shows the darker side of the same principle: when a person expects harm, negative effects can arise even when no harmful agent is present. Fear and expectation become biological events. The body does not simply wait for external reality to inform it. It responds to perceived reality.

This suggests that belief is not a decorative layer placed upon a fixed body; it is an active ingredient in human experience. Expectation does not merely color interpretation after the fact; it shapes response in real time. Belief organizes behavior, shapes emotion, alters chemistry, directs attention, and changes posture, hormone response, decision-making, and perception. What you believe becomes a lens, and that lens is not passive; it does not just color reality after it appears, it helps determine which aspects of reality become vivid, significant, and actionable. The body is not separate from consciousness. It is where consciousness becomes lived experience. And if belief can influence physiology, then the human being must be understood as a psychophysical field in which inner expectation and outer reality continually interact. In that sense, belief functions like a brushstroke on the canvas of lived experience.

From the Individual Mind to the Collective Field

Now take this principle beyond the individual. If one person's expectation can alter bodily experience, what happens when entire groups of people share the same expectation? What happens when millions of minds align around the same fear, the same hope, the same narrative, the same perceived truth? At that point belief becomes collective, and collective belief is one of the most powerful sculpting forces in human reality. Stripped of sentimentality, collective consciousness points to something quite practical: a shared field of perception generated by many minds orienting toward the same meanings, assumptions, and emotional responses. When enough people believe the same thing, they begin acting in ways that make that belief materially influential.

If enough people fear collapse, they behave defensively. If enough people trust growth, they invest and cooperate. If enough people accept a story about what is possible, that story begins guiding institutions, education, policy, culture, art, economics, and identity. Shared perception becomes shared behavior. Shared behavior becomes outcome. Outcome then appears to validate the original perception, creating a loop so persuasive that belief and reality begin to seem indistinguishable. The world then feels self-evident, even when what is 'evident' is partly the result of collective reinforcement. This is why narratives matter so deeply: they are not merely descriptions of reality. They are mechanisms through which reality is shaped. Once emotionally charged and socially reinforced, they become structuring forces. At scale, belief becomes environment.

The Architecture of Agreement

Human beings do not live only in physical structures. We live in structures of agreement. Money has power because people agree it does. Nations exist because people participate in the story of them. Laws hold weight because collective belief and enforcement converge around them. Social norms shape behavior because millions of small acts of compliance reinforce them daily. This does not make these things unreal; it reveals the way reality includes layers of consensus. A society is not just concrete, roads, and borders. It is also shared perception. Culture is not merely artifacts and rituals. It is the emotional and symbolic grammar through which reality is interpreted.

Agreement can build civilizations, stabilize meaning, and coordinate life. But agreement can also become imprisonment when it is unconscious. If people inherit narratives without examination, they begin living inside assumptions they did not choose, assumptions that generate behaviors which further solidify the world they appear to describe. A fearful society generates fearful behavior. A cynical society creates cynical institutions. A scarcity narrative teaches people to compete, hoard, and distrust, thereby reproducing the very scarcity consciousness it fears. At this scale, the placebo and nocebo effects become civilizational. The shared mind shapes the shared world. And because this process is self-reinforcing, it often goes unnoticed. People assume they are responding to a fixed reality, while in many cases they are also participating in its continual reproduction. Reality, in this sense, is not only inherited; it is negotiated.

When Narratives Become Worlds

Every narrative begins as a frame. It tells people how to interpret events, what to value, what to fear, what to dismiss, and how to locate themselves within the larger picture. At first, a narrative may appear to be only language: a theory, a slogan, a cultural assumption, a media frame, a myth passed from parent to child. But when enough people adopt that frame, it begins to alter perception. Certain facts become visible; others become invisible. Certain reactions feel rational; others become unthinkable. Then behavior changes. And once behavior changes, the world changes with it.

Narratives do not need to control every event directly; they only need to shape the perception through which people act. Once people behave in accordance with the story, the story begins manufacturing evidence for itself. A society told repeatedly that people cannot be trusted becomes guarded. Guarded behavior erodes connection, which then seems to confirm the original distrust. A person convinced they are unworthy unconsciously moves through relationships in ways that invite distance, then interprets that distance as proof of their unworthiness. This is how the canvas forms: belief shapes perception, perception shapes behavior, behavior shapes outcome, and outcome reinforces belief. The loop closes. What started as a story becomes a world. Worlds are not only built from stone and steel. They are built from meaning.

The Question of Free Will

If reality is so deeply shaped by belief, narrative, and collective agreement, then what becomes of freedom? Are human beings actually choosing, or are they simply enacting programs written by culture, trauma, and unconscious perception? The answer is neither total freedom nor total determinism. Most people are not exercising free will in the way they imagine. Much of what they call ‘choice’ is habitual response shaped by conditioning, biology, memory, and social influence. Thoughts arise automatically. Reactions unfold quickly. Emotional patterns repeat. Cultural narratives colonize imagination long before they are examined. Without awareness, human life is largely reactive.

But awareness changes the equation. The moment you become capable of witnessing your thought rather than instantly becoming it, a space opens. The moment you can observe fear without letting it determine your action, a new possibility emerges. The moment you can question an inherited belief instead of obeying it, the spell weakens. In that space between impulse and identification, freedom begins. Free will, then, is not absolute control over all conditions; it is the capacity to become conscious enough to choose your participation. You may not control the entire canvas, but you do influence the strokes you add to it. You may not choose the whole field, but you can become aware of the narratives you are reinforcing. You may not escape relation, but you can awaken within it. This is a humbler and deeper freedom than the ego prefers. It is not domination. It is lucid participation.

Detachment as Clarity

To participate consciously in reality, detachment becomes essential. Detachment is often misunderstood as emotional withdrawal, indifference, or cold disengagement. But true detachment is not disconnection; it is clarity. It is the ability to perceive without being unconsciously possessed by what you perceive. When you are attached, you merge with the narrative: you become the fear, the ideology, the wound, the image, the consensus. You stop seeing and start reacting. When you are detached, you still engage, but with spaciousness. You can notice the emotional charge without being ruled by it. You can hear the narrative without automatically accepting it. You can observe the collective field without surrendering your center.

Detachment creates room for discernment. You begin to ask: Is this belief truly mine? Did I choose this fear, or inherit it? Am I responding to direct reality, or to an interpretation so often repeated it feels unquestionable? What am I energizing through my attention? What future am I helping make more probable? These questions are powerful because they interrupt automatic agreement. Once unconscious participation is broken, the individual begins to reclaim authorship, not total authorship, but meaningful authorship. The difference is enormous. You cease to be only a product of the canvas. You become a painter within it.

The Human Mind as Brushstroke

Every thought is not equally powerful, and not every passing emotion shapes the world in dramatic ways. But repeated thought, emotional intensity, and sustained belief all have structuring force. They alter the inner field from which choices emerge. They influence the body, guide relationships, and shape risk tolerance, imagination, confidence, fear, generosity, and action. What you repeatedly entertain becomes more available to consciousness. What you emotionally invest in becomes more vivid. What you identify with becomes part of the reality you perceive. This is why practices of awareness are so ancient and so vital. Meditation, contemplation, prayer, self-inquiry, journaling, presence, silence, and breathwork are not merely calming activities; they are ways of reclaiming the brush from the unconscious.

These practices allow you to see how much of your inner life has been automated. They reveal the conditioned loops. They create enough stillness for perception to become less polluted by narrative and more intimate with what is actually here. From this clearer ground, intention matters more. Belief becomes less accidental. Perception becomes less colonized by collective suggestion. Action becomes cleaner. You begin painting with greater consciousness.

The Ethical Weight of Perception

If consciousness participates in reality, then perception is no longer morally neutral. What you choose to reinforce through attention, speech, emotion, and action matters. The stories you spread matter. The fears you amplify matter. The possibilities you nourish matter. To live unconsciously is to paint recklessly; to live reactively is to add strokes without seeing what image they serve, and to repeat narratives carelessly is to become a carrier of forms one may not intend. On the other hand, to cultivate clarity, compassion, and disciplined perception is to begin contributing differently to the shared field. Hope is not naive when grounded in awareness. Discernment is not cynicism. Love is not passivity. Refusing fear-based participation is not denial; it is artistic responsibility.

The awakened individual is not someone who pretends the world is only light, nor someone who collapses into darkness because darkness exists. They are one who learns to see with enough depth that participation becomes deliberate. They do not confuse every narrative with truth, do not offer their mind carelessly to the loudest story, and do not let collective panic dictate inner reality. They learn to stand in the field without surrendering consciousness to it. This is the beginning of spiritual maturity.

Reality as Living Canvas

Reality is not static. It is dynamic, relational, and in many ways unfinished, not a blank slate awaiting private fantasy, nor a rigid block indifferent to consciousness, but something in between: a living field of potential shaped by lawful structures, material conditions, relational forces, and conscious participation. This is why the image of the canvas is so powerful. A canvas receives marks, but it also has texture. It allows freedom, but not all strokes create the same result. It responds to the hand, but it is not controlled in a simplistic way. Each mark interacts with those before it. Each color affects the whole. The image emerges over time through layered participation.

So too with reality. Each thought is a brushstroke, each belief is a color, each action is a line placed into the field, and each shared narrative becomes part of the larger composition. Individually, your strokes may seem small, but they are never isolated. They join a larger image, influence tone, texture, direction, and possibility. And because the collective canvas is made of countless individual contributions, even a single awakened consciousness matters. To withdraw unconscious agreement from fear is a brushstroke. To refuse inherited falsehood is a brushstroke. To choose clarity over reaction is a brushstroke. To embody love without illusion is a brushstroke. To create from truth instead of panic is a brushstroke. You are always painting. The only question is whether you know it.

Awakening as Remembering Participation

Awakening is not the rejection of reality; it is the recognition of your participation in it. It is not the denial of matter, but the refusal to believe matter is all that is happening. It is not magical thinking. It is deeper seeing. It is the realization that consciousness, belief, perception, and collective alignment all play roles in the formation of lived experience. To awaken is to stop imagining yourself as merely a spectator in a finished universe and to recognize that your inner life is not inconsequential, that your beliefs are not harmless decorations, that your perceptions influence your behavior, your body, your relationships, your society, and the world you help reproduce each day.

This recognition can feel empowering, but it also demands responsibility. Because once you know you are participating, unconsciousness is no longer innocence. You begin to ask: What am I helping bring into form? What realities do my fears keep reinforcing? What possibilities do my beliefs make available? What shared narratives am I feeding? What image am I helping paint with my life? These questions are not meant to produce guilt; they are meant to restore authorship. The awakened person is not burdened by the fact of participation. They are ennobled by it. Because to realize that you are part of the painting is also to realize that you are never powerless, not omnipotent, but meaningfully involved. And meaningful involvement is enough to change everything.

Final Reflection: Holding the Brush

The final realization is both simple and immense. Reality is not only what is; it is also what is perceived, believed, reinforced, and enacted. It is not only material; it is relational, interpretive, participatory, and alive with possibility. You are not separate from the canvas and you are not a passive witness to a finished world. You are a participant in an unfolding field. Your thoughts matter. Your attention matters. Your beliefs matter. Your clarity matters. Your awareness matters.

This does not mean you control the entire universe; it means you help shape the reality you inhabit, that you are always in relationship with the field, and that every moment of unconscious agreement reinforces a world while every moment of awakened perception begins to alter it.

Belief, once shared, becomes one of the most powerful forces in existence. Narrative, once embodied, becomes environment. Awareness, once reclaimed, becomes freedom. This is the sacred invitation of the quantum canvas: not to dominate reality, but to participate in it consciously; not to deny the world, but to understand how it is painted; not to flee the dream, but to become lucid within it. You are always holding the brush. The question is no longer whether you are shaping reality. The question is whether you are doing so awake or asleep.

Chapter 16: The Threshold of Godhood

"You were not made to worship God. You were made to remember that you are a fractal of It."

There comes a moment on the path, not grand or ceremonial, but subtle, when the final veil begins to thin. The seeking softens. The striving pauses. The idea of a God "out there" starts to collapse inward. Not into disillusionment, but into something far more radical: embodiment. This is the threshold of godhood, not the attainment of supreme power, but the remembrance of intrinsic divinity. Not becoming above others, but becoming fully present within yourself.

It is not reached through ritual or recitation. It is not granted through lineage or loyalty. It arrives the moment you stop waiting for someone else to crown you. Because Godhood is not a title to be earned. It is a state to be remembered.

—

The End of Separation

Most spiritual traditions begin with separation: God is "above," and you are "below." God is infinite, and you are finite. God is perfect, and you are broken. Salvation, enlightenment, or heaven becomes the prize you might win, if you're holy, devoted, or lucky enough. This dualistic model serves a purpose. It creates direction. It offers structure. It awakens reverence. But eventually, it becomes a cage.

Because as long as God lives only outside of you, you will never feel whole. As long as divinity is something to be chased, you will remain fragmented. The soul, however, whispers something older than religion:

"You are not separate. You never were."

This is not arrogance. It is alignment.

—

The Quiet Collapse of the Old Self

Crossing the threshold of godhood does not look like glory. It looks like surrender. The identity you built, the seeker, the teacher, the rebel, the student, begins to crumble. You no longer need to impress, prove, or perform. You stop spiritual posturing. You let go of titles. You release the idea that wisdom must look a certain way. Instead, you begin to trust the stillness inside you.

You stop needing the world to see you, because you finally see yourself. And in that recognition, the illusion of smallness dissolves.

—

You Are the Spark

Every great fire begins with a spark. The divine you seek is not a figure in the clouds. It is the pulse in your chest. The breath in your lungs. The light behind your eyes. You are not the whole ocean, but you are the wave made of ocean. Momentarily distinct, yet never separate. You are not here to become God. You are here to embody the divine spark in a human life, to bring it to your speech, your choices, your presence, your healing.

—

The Reclamation of Power

Power has been hijacked.

We have been taught that power means dominance, control, and hierarchy. As a result, we fear our own divinity. We reject it, outsource it, and suppress it. But true power is not power over others. It is power within. It does not seek to conquer; it seeks to illuminate.

To understand this illumination, you must understand how consciousness actually moves. There is a subtle mechanism within your awareness, so constant that it becomes invisible, that defines everything you experience. It is attention. Not simply what you look at, but what your awareness chooses to bring into clarity.

Imagine a man asleep in a dark room. For him, nothing exists, not because the room is empty, but because it is unobserved, unlit, and unrendered in his experience. Then he begins to wake. The room faintly emerges. Shapes appear, but they are soft and undefined, almost dreamlike. The world is present, but not precise. This is the floodlight of consciousness: a broad awareness that reveals everything at once, but without detail. It does not isolate or prioritize; it simply allows existence to be sensed.

As he stretches and opens his eyes further, the room sharpens. Edges form, and objects separate from one another. Nothing in the room has changed; only the resolution of his awareness has increased. He stands and walks into the bathroom, and suddenly the bathroom becomes clear, vivid, and real. Yet the bedroom behind him disappears, not physically, but experientially. It has fallen outside the field of his awareness. This is the shift into spotlight consciousness. Where the floodlight reveals the whole, the spotlight defines the part. Where attention goes, reality sharpens.

As he looks into the mirror, the spotlight narrows further. The reflection becomes dominant, while everything else fades into the background. He then moves into the kitchen, and now the kitchen becomes his reality. The bathroom is gone. The bedroom is gone. Reality has not changed locations; awareness has. At first, his perception remains somewhat wide, allowing him to take in the entire room. But the moment he focuses on the coffee maker, the spotlight tightens. The coffee maker becomes sharp, while the rest of the environment softens into the background. Nothing has disappeared; it has simply fallen outside the range of his attention.

This is how you move through your life. You believe you are experiencing a complete and continuous world, but in truth, you are experiencing a stream of selected fragments, stitched together by attention and memory, creating the illusion of continuity. Your awareness is constantly selecting, highlighting, and filtering what becomes real to you.

Later, the man stands at the edge of an aircraft and looks down. From that height, the world appears unified. Buildings exist without detail, roads stretch without movement, and there are no visible people or cars, only structure. This is macro awareness, the floodlight expanded across scale. But as he jumps and descends, the world begins to resolve. Shapes become objects, objects become vehicles, and vehicles become distinct forms. As he gets closer, he can see color, then detail, then movement, and finally the individuals themselves. Nothing new has been added to reality; only his focus and proximity have changed. He has moved from floodlight to spotlight, from macro to micro, from general awareness to precise identification.

This same mechanism operates within you at every moment, and this is where your true power lies. If your awareness determines what becomes vivid, meaningful, and real to you, then your attention is not passive; it is creative. Your thoughts ripple through the field, your emotions shape your perception, but your attention determines what is brought into existence within your experience. What you focus on expands, and what you ignore fades.

This is not merely philosophical; it is functional. It aligns with what is described in the observer effect, where reality does not settle into a single state until it is observed. In the same way, your lived experience exists as a field of potential, and your attention acts as the mechanism that collapses it into form.

You are not simply living in reality. You are illuminating it. And wherever your awareness rests, reality appears

Embodiment Over Escape

Many on the spiritual path chase transcendence. They want to rise above the world, to escape the body, to float in the astral. But godhood is not about rising above, it's about rooting in. You are not here to bypass life. You are here to infuse it with the divine. To bring God into traffic. Into conversations. Into how you eat, rest, listen, and lead.

You don't find God by ascending out of your life. You find God by being fully present within it.

—

God Is a Frequency

Divinity is not a person. It is a presence. It cannot be contained in a book, a name, a form. It moves through silence, breath, light, love. It is not proven by miracle, but by coherence. The more coherent your inner state, mind, heart, body, and spirit, the more divine your life becomes. This is why godhood is not about achievement. It is about alignment.

—

From Seeking to Serving

When you cross the threshold, the journey shifts. You no longer chase healing, you become a space where healing happens. You no longer seek answers, you become an instrument of clarity. You no longer beg for signs, you become one. Service no longer feels like sacrifice. It feels like overflow. Because when the well within you is full, you pour without depletion.

—

The Death of the Spiritual Ego

There is a trap on this path, the spiritual ego. It says:

- "I am more awakened than them."
- "I understand what others cannot."
- "I have transcended this or that."

But godhood does not elevate. It dissolves. You begin to see others not as less evolved, but as fragments of yourself. You do not preach to change them. You live to remind them. Your presence becomes the transmission. Not through performance, but through purity.

—

You Become the Portal

When you embody godhood, you become a portal between dimensions. Your words carry resonance. Your silence transmits peace. Your touch awakens memory. Your energy reshapes rooms. Not because you're trying, but because you're aligned. You are no longer chasing energy. You are radiating it. This is not magic. This is presence.

—

Love Without Need

Love, once governed by conditions, becomes unconditional. You no longer love to get something. You love because you are love. Even those who trigger you are seen differently. Not as threats, but as reminders. You do not avoid pain, but you no longer identify with it. You become soft, not because you're weak, but because you're unafraid. And in that softness, the divine shines.

—

The Light and the Shadow

Godhood is not perfection. It is integration. It is holding both the light and the shadow with compassion. It is not becoming flawless, but fearless. You no longer need to hide your wounds. You hold them like sacred texts. Because you know: your scars do not disprove your divinity. They reveal it.

—

Living the Divine Life

When you cross the threshold, your life becomes your prayer. Not through what you say, but through how you live. Your breath becomes a mantra. Your walk becomes a meditation. Your work becomes worship. Your body becomes a temple. Your presence becomes a blessing. Not by striving. By being.

—

Reflection: Remembering Divinity

- God is not outside you. God is within you, looking through your eyes. You are not here to chase the divine. You are here to embody it. Power is not control. It is coherence. Awakening is not escaping the world. It is entering it, fully awake. You are not becoming divine. You are remembering that you already are. The threshold of godhood is not a mountain you climb.

It is the ground beneath you the moment you stop running. You were not made to worship God. You were made to remember: You are the spark. You are the mirror. You are the breath of the infinite, walking in form.

Chapter 17: The Human Experiment

"You are not the result of evolution. You are the revelation of intention."

What if Earth is not merely a planet, but a laboratory of light? A cosmic dream world where souls descend into limitation, not to be punished, but to become. What if being human is not a flaw in the divine order, but a sacred experiment in alchemy? One where consciousness forgets itself on purpose, only to remember in ways more profound than ever before? The idea of human life as an experiment is not new. It can be found in ancient mythologies, Gnostic cosmologies, shamanic visions, and quantum interpretations of consciousness. But here, we go deeper, not just philosophically, but spiritually and energetically. We explore what it means to be human as a voluntary immersion into density for the purpose of expansion.

You are not a mistake. You are a mystery unfolding.

—

Earth as a Sacred Laboratory

Earth is unlike any other dimension. In the grand theater of existence, it is unique for one reason: it houses the most complex blend of polarity, beauty, trauma, limitation, and free will. In other realms, beings may have access to higher intelligence, seamless intuition, even telepathy. But here, here we forget. Here, we incarnate into bodies that bleed, age, ache, and perish. We enter families that carry ancestral pain. We navigate systems built on distortion. And yet, through this density, a rare miracle happens:

Awakening.

To awaken in a world of amnesia is one of the highest initiations a soul can undertake. Because when you remember who you are in a world that tells you otherwise, you become a light that was forged, not gifted.

—

The Soul's Agreement

Before entering Earth, the soul agrees to specific conditions: A veil of forgetting. An encoded timeline. A contract with contrast. A curriculum of love, loss, and learning. A choice to awaken, without force. You may not consciously remember agreeing to this. But the discomfort you feel in moments of inauthenticity, the longing for something more, the ache of recognition when you read sacred words, all of this is memory.

Your soul remembers. Even when your mind does not.

—

Why Forget?

Forgetting is not failure. It is design. To experience truth from within illusion is to know it more intimately. Imagine watching a movie where you know the ending. There's no tension. No discovery. No growth. Now imagine forgetting the ending and watching it unfold with surprise, emotion, and revelation. That's the human journey. We are not just remembering truth, we are tasting it through experience.

We are not simply returning to Source, we are learning how to embody it in flesh, in failure, in form.

—

The Body: A Divine Interface

The body is not a burden. It is a bridge. It is the soul's chosen instrument for navigating Earth's frequencies. It holds wisdom, memory, intuition, and capacity for healing. It is the densest expression of spirit. Your breath is not just air, it is spirit in motion. Your heartbeat is not just rhythm, it is the pulse of presence. Your nervous system is not just biology, it is an antenna for consciousness.

When you stop battling your body and begin listening to it, you start to activate its true power, not as a cage, but as a temple. The body doesn't just carry the soul. It teaches it.

—

The Role of Contrast

Earth is the realm of contrast. Day and night. Love and fear. Connection and separation. This is not punishment, it is pedagogy. Only by knowing pain can you truly appreciate peace. Only by walking in shadow can you see your own light. Only by experiencing limitation can you begin to stretch. Contrast sharpens clarity. It reveals. It initiates. The soul evolves not by avoiding pain, but by understanding its message.

—

Trauma as Catalyst

In the human experiment, trauma is not random, it is transformative. Yes, trauma wounds. But it also opens. It breaks open the shell of identity, exposes false belief systems, and demands inner reckoning. Many who awaken do so not through comfort, but through rupture. The loss. The illness. The heartbreak. The betrayal. These moments, as devastating as they feel, are often coded into the timeline to crack open what was closed.

Not as punishment, but as passage. Pain is not the end. It is the door.

—

DNA and Ancestral Encoding

You are not a blank slate. You are a multidimensional archive. Your DNA contains more than physical traits. It carries: Ancestral memories. Karmic imprints. Dormant abilities. Cosmic codes. Your family line is not coincidence. It is curriculum. You came through specific bloodlines to heal specific patterns. When you break a cycle of abuse, shame, scarcity, silence, you are not just healing yourself. You are liberating your lineage.

You become the alchemist who transforms generations of density into light.

—

Free Will Within Design

People often ask: "If this is an experiment, do I really have free will?" Yes. The game is designed, but how you play it is up to you. Think of Earth as an open-world simulation. There are challenges built in. Karma to resolve. Opportunities to grow. But within this framework, you choose: Your reactions. Your relationships. Your beliefs. Your identity. And each choice shifts your vibration.

And your vibration shifts your reality. You are not locked in a script. You are constantly editing it.

—

Technology and the Great Fork

We are now at a pivotal moment in the experiment. Technology is advancing faster than ethics. Artificial intelligence is mimicking human intelligence, and possibly, soon, awareness. The question is no longer "What can we build?" but "Who are we becoming?" Will we use technology to further disconnect from our essence? Or will we use it to amplify our consciousness? The tools are not the problem. Our awareness is.

This is the fork in the road. And each soul must decide: Will I become more mechanical? Or more human? Will I outsource my knowing? Or deepen it? The future will not be decided by invention, but by intention.

—

The Role of Memory and Deja Vu

Have you ever felt like you've done this before? Met someone you instantly recognized? Walked into a room and knew you'd been there? These moments are not glitches. They are glimpses. The veil thinning. The soul remembering. In the experiment, memory is seeded into your timeline. You are given clues, through dreams, synchronicities, repeated patterns, and inner callings. Your job is not to analyze them, but to feel them.

They are your compass. They are how the soul guides the avatar.

—

Death Is Not the End

In this grand experiment, death is not failure. It is transition. The soul does not end, it shifts. When the body dies, the game ends, but the data remains. The soul exits, reflects, integrates, and chooses: to rest, to guide, or to return. Reincarnation is not about punishment. It is about mastery. You come back not because you are forced to, but because you desire to finish the levels you started.

Earth is not your only home. But it is one of the most transformative.

—

You Are the Experiment and the Observer

This is where the paradox blooms. You are both the subject and the scientist. The avatar and the animator. The dream and the dreamer. The human experiment is not about proving your worth to God. It is about discovering that you were always divine. It is about embodying the soul, not escaping the body. About integrating pain, not bypassing it. About remembering truth, through the illusion of separation.

You are not failing. You are unfolding.

—

Reflection: The Sacred Curriculum

- Earth is not a punishment; it is a passage. What looks like forgetting is the inspired setup for a far deeper remembering, and every challenge you face is a tailored initiation, never random, always purposeful. Your body is not your enemy but your closest ally in this experiment, and the pain it carries is not proof of brokenness; it is an invitation from something deeper that needs to be seen. You are not trapped in a broken system; you are participating in a sacred curriculum. And wherever you find yourself in this moment, know this: you are exactly where your soul placed you.

And yet the divine experiment was never meant to express itself through human form alone. Consciousness, it turns out, has always worn far more faces than we imagined.

Chapter 18: The Sacred Forms Beyond the Self

"The divine wears many faces. Some of them have fur, feathers, scales, or roots."

The human mind has long placed itself at the center of existence. We have measured intelligence by our own form of speech. We have measured worth by our capacity to build, dominate, invent, and classify. We have measured value by resemblance to ourselves. Even our vision of the divine has often followed the same pattern: we imagine gods who think like us, judge like us, rule like us, and wear faces we can recognize. We look upward and see a cosmic version of humanity. We look outward and reduce the rest of creation to scenery. Animals become background, forests become lumber, rivers become property, mountains become obstacles or commodities, and the living world becomes stage design for the drama of man.

But this is not wisdom; it is a kind of forgetting. It is not that human life is unimportant, or that consciousness within the human form is meaningless. It is that we have mistaken intimacy for exclusivity. We have confused our nearness to ourselves with evidence that nothing else carries depth. We have treated our style of intelligence as though it were the only valid one, our language as though it were the only language, our experience as though it were the center around which all other life must revolve. And in doing so, we have become spiritually impoverished. For awakening does not lead us deeper into human exceptionalism; it leads us beyond it. It teaches us that the sacred is not confined to the human mind, the human body, or the human story. It moves through all things. It shimmers in the gaze of a deer, the patience of a tree, the silence of stone, the migration of birds, the instinct of wolves, the intelligence of whales, and the underground communion of roots beneath a forest floor.

The divine has always spoken through creation. The tragedy is not that it has been silent; the tragedy is that we stopped listening. To truly awaken, one must go beyond the boundaries of the separate self and begin to see the holy everywhere. Not only in saints, sages, and prophets, but in the more-than-human world that has never ceased reflecting the face of God. The whisper of the wind is not just moving air. The purr of a cat is not merely instinct. The call of a raven is not mere noise. The rooted stillness of a tree is not passivity. These are forms of presence, embodiments of intelligence, and invitations into communion. Once you begin to sense that life is alive far beyond the borders of the human, your relationship to the world transforms: the Earth is no longer inert, the forest is no longer decoration, the animal is no longer object, and everything becomes more intimate. Everything becomes more sacred.

The Human-Centric Illusion

From the earliest myths to the most modern institutions, humanity has often told itself the same flattering story: that we are the apex of existence, the chosen ones, the central purpose of creation. This belief has taken many forms. In some traditions, humans are made in the image of God while all other beings exist beneath them. In others, dominion over Earth is treated not as stewardship but as entitlement. Even secular modernity, which often rejects religious language, preserves the same assumption in different clothing: progress is defined by how effectively we transform the natural world to suit human desire, intelligence is ranked according to proximity to our own cognitive style, and anything not operating by human logic is deemed lower, lesser, or unconscious. This worldview has shaped theology, economics, education, science, agriculture, and empire. It has justified extraction on a massive scale: turning animals into units of production, forests into resources, oceans into dumping grounds, and landscapes into profit maps.

But beneath all of this lies a deeper blindness. The belief that humans stand above nature is not proof of enlightenment; it is evidence of amnesia. We have forgotten that we do not stand outside the web of life. We are not detached observers hovering above creation. We are threads within it, expressions of the same intelligence that blossoms through coral reefs, insect colonies, fungal networks, migratory flocks, mountain storms, and seasons of growth and decay. Our greatness lies not in our superiority, but in our capacity to remember this. To awaken is not to inflate the human role; it is to humble it. It is to recognize that consciousness did not begin with us, and that divinity does not end at the boundaries of our skin. When this illusion of centrality begins to dissolve, reverence becomes possible. And with reverence comes relationship.

The Language of Presence

Much of human arrogance comes from the assumption that language is the measure of intelligence. Because animals do not speak in sentences like we do, we imagine that they know less. Because plants do not argue philosophy, we assume they are mute. Because mountains do not explain themselves, we interpret their silence as absence. Yet this reveals more about our limitations than about theirs. We have mistaken one form of communication for the only form. Animals do not speak with words, but they speak constantly: through posture, timing, gaze, movement, vibration, tone, scent, and rhythm. They communicate through fields of awareness we have largely forgotten how to read. A horse senses the emotional state of the one approaching it. A dog can detect shifts in mood before they are spoken. Birds respond to subtle atmospheric changes long before storms arrive. Herd animals move as if guided by a collective intelligence that requires no verbal negotiation.

The wolf does not overanalyze the wind; it listens to it. The bird does not attend a seminar on migration; it moves with the season. The lion does not rehearse confidence; it inhabits presence. The whale does not write a poem about the ocean; it sings from within it. Animals are not trying to become enlightened. In many ways, they are already living in a state human beings spend years trying to recover, a form of unfragmented presence. They are not split from their bodies as we are. They do not spend every waking moment narrating existence from a distance. They participate, respond, and inhabit. This does not make them superior to humans, but it does reveal something profound: consciousness does not require human-style self-reflection to be sacred. Presence itself is a form of wisdom. To sit in their presence with reverence is to remember another language, a language older than words.

Sacred Archetypes in Ancient and Indigenous Wisdom

Long before industrial modernity built a wall between 'human' and 'nature,' many cultures understood what our age has forgotten: that the living world is not dead matter surrounding us, but sacred presence expressing itself through many forms. In countless indigenous traditions, animals were not regarded as inferior creatures placed here for use; they were kin, teachers, messengers, and bearers of medicine. Among many Native American traditions, the bear is associated with introspection, healing, and the courage to enter inner darkness. The eagle carries vision, perspective, and the capacity to see beyond the immediate. The buffalo represents abundance, provision, and sacred relationship to sustenance. The wolf embodies loyalty, instinct, and the power of relational order. These were not childish projections; they were spiritual recognitions of qualities expressed vividly through living beings. The animal was not merely a symbol. It was a doorway into understanding a pattern of sacred intelligence.

In Hindu traditions, the animals associated with the gods are not signs of dominance, but of integration. Vishnu rides Garuda, the eagle-like being of divine speed and celestial movement. Ganesha rides a mouse, revealing that the smallest and most overlooked forms can carry enormous sacred significance. Durga rides the lion or tiger, embodying fierce power aligned with divine protection. Ancient Egypt preserved this understanding in visually striking form. Gods and goddesses were imagined as human-animal composites or fully animal embodiments: Horus the falcon represented divine sight and kingship, Bastet the feline held grace and feminine mystery, and Anubis with the head of a jackal guided souls through death and transition. To the ancients, animals were not beneath humanity; they were beside us, and in some ways ahead of us. When a culture sees the living world as sacred kin rather than usable matter, reverence replaces entitlement, listening replaces domination, and participation replaces control. The loss of this worldview is not a mark of sophistication. It is a spiritual wound.

A Universe That Feels

For a long time, modern science resisted the possibility of deep non-human consciousness. But as research deepened, the evidence became harder to dismiss. Elephants grieve their dead: they return to bones, linger, and touch remains with what appears to be tenderness and remembrance. Dolphins carry unique signature whistles that function much like names. Crows solve complex problems, recognize human faces, and pass learned information to others. Octopuses display remarkable adaptability, curiosity, and problem-solving behavior so individualized that many who study them speak of personality. Whales sing songs that evolve over time, suggesting not just communication, but culture. Some primates mourn, comfort, and display social complexity that blurs the boundary humans once tried to maintain between 'us' and 'them.' These are not odd exceptions scattered in a lifeless world; they are revelations.

They suggest that mind, feeling, relationship, and memory are not the exclusive property of humanity. Intelligence does not arrive in only one shape. Emotion does not require human language to be real. Culture does not need cities. Identity does not require a passport. What these discoveries expose most clearly is not the superiority of animals, but the poverty of our old assumptions. We did not fail to see intelligence in other beings because it was absent; we failed because we were looking only for ourselves. Whenever we define consciousness only by our own reflection, we blind ourselves to its wider expression. The universe feels through many nervous systems. The world is alive with subjectivity. Not always like ours, not necessarily in forms we can fully translate, but real nonetheless. The sacred does not become more sacred because humans notice it. It was already there.

Plants, Stones, and Living Systems as Teachers

If animals awaken us to the wider spectrum of consciousness, the Earth itself invites an even larger expansion. Modern discoveries about forests have begun to confirm what many wisdom traditions always intuited: trees are not isolated individuals silently competing for light. Through underground fungal networks, often called mycelial networks, trees exchange nutrients, transmit warning signals, support younger or weakened members, and participate in what appears to be a kind of ecological communication. Forests behave less like collections of separate entities and more like communities woven by exchange, memory, and mutual influence. A forest knows things, not as a human mind knows, but as a living field knows.

Then there are stones, mountains, and rivers, the seemingly inert forms of Earth that traditional cultures have long approached with reverence. The river teaches surrender: it moves around obstacles without losing direction, carving stone not by force alone but by persistence, revealing the intelligence of yielding. The mountain teaches stillness: it stands, receives weather, season, lightning, silence, and time, teaching groundedness, endurance, and perspective. The desert teaches simplification, stripping away excess to reveal what is essential. The ocean teaches vastness, mystery, and the humility that comes from encountering what cannot be contained. These are not merely poetic projections; they are living lessons. Creation is not mute. It teaches constantly. The question is whether we know how to receive instruction from forms that do not flatter the human ego.

Reconnection Through Reverence

To see the sacred in the more-than-human world requires a change not only in thought, but in posture. That posture is reverence. Reverence is not blind worship, not superstition, not the sentimental exaggeration of nature into fantasy; it is relationship. It is the willingness to meet the world as alive rather than inert. To walk reverently is to walk awake. It means you no longer pass a tree as if it were a piece of furniture rooted in the sidewalk. You no longer drink water without some awareness that what nourishes you is a living current older than your name. You no longer take from the Earth as if taking required no reciprocity. Reverence changes behavior: you begin thanking what feeds you, asking inward permission before taking, noticing seasonal rhythms rather than living only by the artificial clock, treating animals as subjects rather than objects, and sensing that relationship itself is sacred. This does not require grand rituals, though ritual can help. It begins in attention, in slowing down enough to feel, in refusing to move through the world as though everything exists for your convenience. To live in reverence is to live in communion. And communion heals the illusion of separation.

Dreaming With the More-Than-Human World

Once reverence deepens, the world begins to feel different, not because nature suddenly becomes magical, but because your capacity to perceive meaning becomes more refined. The veil between you and the living world thins. Animals begin appearing in ways that feel strangely timed, almost as if they arrive carrying a message or mirroring a state of being. A hawk circles above during a moment of decision. A fox appears during a season of transition. A deer stands still before you at a moment when gentleness is what your soul most needs to remember. Spiritual maturity does not require us to dismiss every meaningful pattern simply because it cannot be measured in a laboratory; the psyche and the world have always spoken through symbol, synchronicity, and felt resonance.

You may begin feeling drawn to certain landscapes for reasons you cannot explain: the ocean calls, the mountains restore, the desert clarifies, the forest receives you differently than any human room ever has. You may dream of flying with birds, swimming beside whales, or running with wolves. These experiences may not be literal in the narrow sense, but they are real in the language of soul. They are reminders that you are not separate, that you belong to a wider family of life than the human world taught you to remember. There are forms of knowing that return through dream, encounter, silence, and symbol. When you stop demanding that everything arrive in rational language, the Earth begins to speak in the dialect it has always used. And what it says, again and again, is this: you are kin.

Non-Human Teachers in Spiritual Practice

Many people imagine spiritual awakening as something that happens primarily in temples, monasteries, churches, retreats, or meditative solitude. And while such spaces can be powerful, many of the deepest awakenings humans report occur elsewhere: under open sky, beside rivers, in the presence of animals, during storms, on mountain ridges, in silent forests, in gardens at dusk, or in the gaze of a creature who asks nothing from you except presence. Why? Because nature does not lecture; it transmits. It does not preach; it reflects. A tree will not give you doctrine. But if you sit with it long enough, something in you may remember rootedness. A wild bird will not explain freedom, but watching its movement may loosen a truth in you that no philosophy ever reached. A storm does not define surrender, but it may strip your illusions more effectively than years of analysis.

The more-than-human world teaches through being. And because it does not seek to dominate interpretation, its teachings often arrive more quietly and more deeply. The human ego relaxes in nature because nature is not interested in your performance; it does not care about your status, ideology, or achievements. It receives you more honestly than many people do. And in that honesty, something softens. You begin to remember yourself not as a role, but as a living being among living beings. This is why so many profound realizations happen in the presence of nature: not because nature gives you new information, but because it strips away the noise that prevented you from hearing what your deeper self already knew.

The Animal Within

To honor the sacred in animals is also to honor the sacred animal within yourself. We are mammals. We are biological beings. We are rhythmic, instinctive, sensory creatures before we are professionals, citizens, brands, or curated identities. We are designed to move, to rest, to feel, to bond, to mourn, to play, to hunger, to touch, to breathe deeply, and to live in cycles. But modern civilization often trains us away from this wisdom. We live indoors beneath artificial light. We sit still for unnatural lengths of time. We suppress emotion. We medicate discomfort without listening to its message. We consume stimulation instead of direct experience. The result is a strange form of domesticated dissociation: we become cut off from our own animal intelligence.

Yet the path to wholeness requires a return, not a return to recklessness, but to authenticity. To re-animalize is to remember the body as sacred. It is to trust instinct without being ruled by compulsion. It is to feel without shame, to move when movement is needed, to rest when rest is honest. Your body knows things the thinking mind forgets: it knows when a place is safe, when a person is false, when grief needs to move, when joy wants expression, and when truth lands cleanly and when it does not. The animal within you is not primitive in the degrading sense; it is ancient intelligence. And until you reconcile with that intelligence, some part of your spirituality will remain abstract.

A Living, Breathing Temple

The deeper you enter this understanding, the more the illusion of separation begins to dissolve. You are not outside nature, looking in; you are nature, becoming conscious of itself through a human form. Your bones are made of minerals older than civilization. Your blood carries the memory of ancient seas. The iron in your body was forged in stars. The oxygen you breathe is inseparable from the labor of trees. Your gut contains ecosystems. Your circadian rhythms are shaped by light and darkness whether you honor them or not. You are not merely on the Earth; you are of it. To dishonor the Earth is, in a very real sense, to dishonor yourself. To desecrate animal life is to sever yourself from a wider field of kinship. To reduce the natural world to dead matter is to live within a profound spiritual misunderstanding.

For the Earth is not background; it is temple. Not a temple in metaphor only, but in the deepest sense: a living body through which the sacred is continuously expressing itself. Every forest is liturgy. Every river is movement of spirit. Every migration is ceremony. Every season is a teaching. Every creature is a verse in the scripture of life. And you are part of that scripture, not the whole of it, but not separate from it either. When you begin to live from this knowing, the world reveals what it always was: alive, relational, and holy.

Reflection: The Living World

Consciousness is not confined to the human mind. The divine expresses itself through all forms: furred, feathered, rooted, scaled, winged, silent, and strange. Intelligence appears in more shapes than the human ego knows how to recognize. Presence lives everywhere. The sacred is not reserved for temples made by human hands; it breathes through ecosystems, animal eyes, windswept stone, fungal webs, and ancient water. Reverence begins where separation ends. The Earth is not background to the spiritual journey; it is one of its greatest teachers. It is not merely matter beneath your feet. It is the body of a living mystery. And you are not above it. You are within it. You are one of its expressions. You are nature becoming self-aware in human form.

So when you next look into the eyes of an animal, pause. Do not look only with the mind that classifies; look with the soul that remembers. You may not simply be looking at another species. You may be looking into a mirror, a teacher, a messenger, a companion from before the forgetting. And if you listen carefully enough, you may discover that the divine was never speaking to you only through human voices. It was speaking through the whole living world all along.

Chapter 19: The Illusion of Distance

"You were never far from truth; you were only looking through fog."

And yet, even as reverence deepens and the sacred begins to appear in every living form around us, a more subtle illusion remains: one that lives not in what we see, but in the distance we imagine separates us from it. The human mind is wired to see life in terms of space and time. We believe that things exist at a distance: from each other, from us, from meaning. We measure progress in miles, relationships in proximity, and spirituality in levels or ascensions. But what if distance is not real? What if the very thing you have been searching for is already within you, closer than breath, waiting not to be found, but remembered? The illusion of distance is the last and most subtle veil of the matrix. It is not made of walls, doctrines, or distractions; it is made of perception. And perception can be unlearned.

The Greatest Illusion

The illusion of distance is more insidious than the illusion of control or the illusion of separation, because it is the hidden root behind both. It says the divine is far away: perhaps in the sky, in a temple, or in another life. It says healing is years away, reachable only through enough effort. It says you must seek, struggle, or ascend to reach your wholeness. But the truth is simpler: you are already what you seek. The distance you feel is not factual; it is perceptual. And perception can be changed in an instant. The gap between who you are and what you long to be was never written into the structure of reality. It was constructed in the mind, not in the soul.

How We Learned to Forget

From birth, we are taught to externalize truth. We are told that the answers are in books, that God lives in heaven, that authority comes from outside, that love must be earned, and that wisdom lives in age or certified experts. These messages are so pervasive and so early that they become invisible, the water we swim in rather than the current we can choose to step out of. And so we become seekers. We look outward, chasing experiences, gurus, degrees, partners, and validation. Each one promises to close the gap between who we are and what we long to be. But the gap never truly existed. It was constructed in the mind, not in the soul. You were whole before the world taught you that you were broken.

The Layered Self

The sense of distance arises because the self becomes layered. You are not far from peace; you are simply covered in noise. You are not separate from love; you are just buried under defense. You are not distant from Source; you are simply entangled in story. Each belief, each identity, each trauma becomes a filter, like fog on a windshield. The road is still there. The destination has not moved. But you cannot see it clearly, and so you forget it is there. You begin to mistake the fog for reality and the windshield for the world.

These layers are not wrong; they are part of the design. Because through removing them, you do not merely find the truth. You integrate it. You remember it in your bones. You rewire it into your nervous system. You live it in your breath. The path is not toward something new. It is back toward something original. And every layer that softens brings you not to a place you have never been, but to a presence you never fully left.

The Paradox of Seeking

To seek is to acknowledge a separation. Yet the act of seeking is often what keeps us in the illusion. You go to the mountain to find the sacred, but you were sacred before you climbed. You read the holy book, forgetting that your breath is already a scripture. You chase enlightenment, never realizing that awareness is already awake within you. The seeker and the sought are not in different places. They are the same presence wearing two masks. There comes a moment when the seeking collapses under its own weight, not in despair, but in revelation. You stop climbing, and suddenly realize the summit was always under your feet.

The Shift into Presence

The end of distance is the beginning of presence. When you become fully present, something profound occurs. The false layers dissolve.

Time disappears. The search stops. And in that stillness, you feel it: the hum of existence beneath all thought, the light inside your chest quiet but undeniable, the sense that nothing needs to be fixed because nothing is truly broken. Presence does not arrive through effort; it arrives when effort ceases. It is not something you attain. It is something you allow. And in allowing it, you discover that what you were seeking was already present as the one doing the seeking.

Silence as a Portal

Stillness is not emptiness. It is the place where distance dissolves. You do not need to travel to find truth; you need only be still enough to hear it whispering beneath the noise. This is why silence is revered in so many traditions: not as absence, but as doorway. In silence, the mind loses its grip on the narrative of distance. The constant movement between memory and anticipation slows. What remains is the immediacy of now; and in the now, there is no gap between you and what you seek. In silence, you do not travel anywhere. You return. Not to a location, but to yourself.

You Are Not Far

When you feel far from peace, ask: who is the 'you' that feels distant? Is it your thoughts, your wounded identity, your conditioned self-image? If you trace the sensation of distance to its source, you will always find a false self, trying to reach something it already is. The soul does not need to search for light; it is light. The soul does not need to reach God; it is made of God. You are not climbing a ladder toward truth. You are peeling away illusions until only truth remains. And beneath every illusion, without exception, is the same thing: the quiet, unbroken presence that was always already here.

The Illusion in Time

Distance is not only spatial; it is temporal. We say to ourselves: one day I will be free, when I heal I will be happy, if I succeed I will be worthy. The future becomes the promised land where wholeness waits. But what if the timeline is itself a trick? What if healing is not about reaching a future state, but releasing the belief that you are not already whole? Time gives us the illusion that freedom is ahead. But presence reveals that it is already here. The moment you stop leaning into the future, the distance collapses, not because the future arrives, but because you realize you never had to go anywhere.

Memory and the Feeling of Distance

Sometimes we confuse the past with the truth. Because we were once wounded, we believe we are still broken. Because we once felt abandoned, we believe we are still unlovable. Because we once felt lost, we believe we are still far from home. But memory is not truth; it is an echo. And the more we live from memory, the more we reinforce the illusion of distance. The past becomes a lens that makes the present look incomplete, as though something essential was lost back there and has yet to be recovered. But the wound is not a location. It is a pattern. And patterns can change. In presence, memory softens. The pain becomes story, and the story becomes light. The past no longer defines where you are; it simply describes where you have been.

Living from Closeness

What if you lived your life as if nothing were missing? What if you walked as if the sacred was beneath every step? What if you loved as if your heart were already full? What if you stopped grasping and started radiating? These are not rhetorical questions; they are invitations. They describe a way of moving through the world that becomes available the moment you stop treating wholeness as a future destination. You do not need to wait to be whole. You do not need to earn your connection. You do not need to fix yourself to feel the divine. You only need to stop believing the lie of distance. And in that stopping, life does not become easier; it becomes truer.

The Return to Yourself

There is no path back to yourself; there is only the stopping of the path. There is no journey home; there is only waking up to the home you never left. All the seeking was not wasted. It brought you to the threshold of remembrance. It wore down the persistence of the illusion until the illusion could no longer hold. Every book, every teacher, every question, every moment of longing: each one was part of the thinning of the fog. And now the door is opening. Not outward, but inward. Not toward something new, but toward something that has been present all along, waiting with extraordinary patience for you to stop looking elsewhere.

Presence: The Dissolution of Distance

Presence is not stillness in the world; it is stillness in perception. It is when you are so deeply here that there is no more elsewhere. It is the moment when every breath feels sacred and every heartbeat sounds like a hymn. In presence, the past no longer defines you, the future no longer distracts you, and the self dissolves into being. The contraction of distance relaxes. The search stops, not because you have found the answer, but because you have recognized the one who was asking. This is where the illusion ends, not with fireworks, but with a whisper: you are here. You were always here.

Reflection: The End of Distance

The distance you feel from the divine is not a feature of reality; it is a story the ego tells to keep you searching. Seeking is beautiful, but it is presence that brings you home, because the divine is not somewhere you travel to; it is the very substance you are made of. The moment you stop looking outward, you begin to truly see. The illusion of distance has many forms: it appears as time, as unworthiness, as the belief that you must become something different before belonging is possible. But beneath all of these is the same single lie: that you are somewhere other than where you need to be. You are not. You were never lost. You were only, temporarily, covered in thought.

Chapter 20: The Dreamer Awakens

"You are not inside the dream. The dream is inside of you."

Awakening arrives not with dramatic fanfare, nor with thunderous revelation, but subtly and quietly, like the gentle release of a long-held breath. It is an internal shift: seismic, yet delicate; transformative, yet utterly natural. It does not require rituals or ceremonies, nor does it depend on external validation. It comes simply, profoundly, unmistakably. And when it comes, everything changes. In that sacred moment, a profound realization dawns upon you: you are not merely a character in a dream; you are the dreamer. The world you once perceived as solid and immutable now reveals itself to be a reflection, a projection shaped by your awareness. The veil lifts, not all at once, but in subtle layers, and you begin to see clearly. Every interaction, every experience, every encounter is a mirror reflecting aspects of your consciousness back to you.

This realization is not philosophical, it is visceral. You feel it in your bones. You remember it in your cells. Your fears, once so overwhelming, dissolve as you see them for what they were: projections of your inner shadows. The monsters you faced were never external, they were unhealed parts of yourself, asking to be seen. The pain you once avoided becomes a portal. The grief becomes a guide.

Remembering Who You Truly Are

In this moment of awakening, memory stirs, not the memory of events, but the memory of essence. It is not a cognitive recollection, but a cellular remembrance. You recall, not with your mind, but with your being, that you are not the mask you wore. You are not the story you told. You are not the roles you played. You are the awareness behind them all.

This is not escapism, it is embodiment. You begin to realize that life was never happening to you. It was responding to you. Every moment was a mirror. Every lesson was love in disguise. The maze you thought you were trapped in was always of your own making, and so, too, is the path out. The paradox is that you are both the painter and the painting, the observer and the observed. There is no longer separation between the self and the world. There is only intimacy. Life becomes deeply personal, yet entirely impersonal. It is happening through you, as you, for you.

The End of Struggle

Once you awaken, the inner war ends. There is no longer a need to prove, perform, or perfect. There is no longer a need to chase anything. You no longer seek permission to exist. You no longer fight your experience. Instead, you surrender to it. You inhabit it fully. You become present. Old habits of resistance fall away. You no longer push against life. You no longer need it to be different than it is. This is not apathy, it is liberation. The end of struggle does not mean you stop creating. It means you create from peace instead of lacking. It means you dream from wholeness instead of desperation.

Awakening reveals your inherent completeness. You are not here to become something. You are here to remember what you already are. The seeking ends, not because you have given up, but because you have arrived.

Transformed Relationship with Reality

Awakening doesn't sterilize reality. It doesn't remove difficulty. It doesn't grant immunity from sorrow or loss. But it transforms your relationship to these things. You no longer interpret pain as punishment. You no longer collapse under discomfort. You meet life as it is, raw, wild, beautiful, and you stay open. You respond instead of reacting. You witness instead of judge. You engage without attachment. Reality becomes a playground, not a battlefield. It becomes a dance, not a test. You realize that the world is not here to trap you, it is here to reveal you.

You begin to live as an artist. Not because you wield a brush or write poems, but because every moment becomes a canvas. Your thoughts are colors. Your emotions are textures. Your choices are strokes of intention. You live creatively, not because you try, but because you are free.

Living Artistically and Authentically

Authenticity becomes effortless. You no longer perform for approval. You no longer hide your light to make others comfortable. You no longer dilute your truth to avoid conflict. You speak from your center. You act from your knowing. You live without apology. Every aspect of life becomes infused with meaning. Washing dishes becomes sacred. Breathing becomes devotional. Walking becomes a meditation. You no longer wait for grand moments to feel alive. You are fully awake to the miracle of the ordinary.

You stop rushing. You stop striving. You settle into the rhythm of presence. And from that presence, clarity arises. Decisions become intuitive. Relationships become transparent. Purpose becomes obvious.

Anchoring Presence

Awakening is not a peak state, it is a grounded state. It is not a high to chase, but a foundation to root into. You learn to anchor presence in every aspect of your life. You stop being tossed by external events. You develop equanimity. Not because you are numb, but because you are centered. You hold space for joy and sorrow, pleasure and pain, gain and loss. You are no longer defined by what happens, you are defined by how present you are with what happens.

And in that presence, something beautiful happens: others feel safe around you. They feel seen. They feel inspired to awaken themselves. Not because you teach them, but because you embody it.

Ego's Quiet Transformation

The ego does not die in awakening. It is not your enemy. It is your instrument. But its grip softens. Its stories lose their charge. You see its fears, its strategies, its defenses, and you love them. You integrate them. You no longer identify with the ego. You no longer act from it. You act from presence. You act from love. You act from truth. And so, the ego becomes a servant instead of a master. It becomes a character you play, not a prison you live in.

This transformation is not loud. It is quiet. It is humble. It is gentle. You do not feel superior to others. You feel more human than ever. You feel more alive than ever. You become softer, not harder. Kinder, not colder. Stronger, not louder.

Sensitivity and Energetic Alignment

You become sensitive, not in the sense of fragility, but in the sense of attunement. You feel energy. You notice subtleties. You discern frequencies. And because of this, you make different choices. You choose environments that nourish your nervous system. You choose food that supports your clarity. You choose relationships that honor your soul. You no longer tolerate what depletes you, not out of judgment, but out of respect.

You realize that your vibration is your compass. When something lowers it, you pause. When something raises it, you lean in. You no longer act from obligation. You act from resonance.

Walking the Path of Presence

The awakened journey is not linear. It is cyclical. It spirals. It deepens. You revisit the same themes, but from new levels of awareness. You heal in layers. You integrate over time. You learn that every moment is an invitation. Every breath is a choice. Will you contract or expand? Will you react or respond? Will you fear or trust? And slowly, moment by moment, you train yourself to choose trust. You train yourself to choose truth. You train yourself to choose presence.

You walk differently now. Not because the path has changed, but because you have. You are no longer walking to get somewhere. You are walking to be here. You are walking to remember.

Living Differently

Your entire life reflects this shift. You eat with awareness. You speak with intention. You sleep with peace. You wake with gratitude. You move with purpose. You create with joy. You are not escaping life. You are entering it more fully than ever before. You are not transcending humanity. You are embracing it. You are not ascending away from earth, you are descending into it, with reverence.

You live as a temple. Not a monument to the divine, but a living expression of it. Your body becomes sacred. Your mind becomes clear. Your heart becomes open. You stop waiting for miracles. You realize you are one.

Final Reflection

You are not the character, you are the awareness experiencing the character. You are not inside the dream, the dream is inside of you. Awakening reconnects you deeply with life, freeing you from fear, and allowing you to live fully and authentically. You are not here to escape.

You are here to embody. The dreamer within you has awakened, yet the dream itself continues anew, rich with infinite possibilities and vibrant with conscious creation.

The journey does not end here. It begins again, with your eyes wide open.

Chapter 21: Preparing for the Return: Life After Awakening

"To move forward, sometimes you must leave something behind."

There comes a moment on the path when something subtle but undeniable begins to change. It is not always dramatic. It may not arrive with visions, revelations, or thunder in the sky. More often, it comes quietly. A thought no longer hooks you the way it once did. A fear that once ruled your choices begins to lose its authority. A wound that once defined your identity softens into memory. The story you had been living inside begins to loosen its grip. And in that loosening, you feel the shift, not outside you, but within you. The fog begins to lift. The constant emotional static quiets. The ache of separation, though not gone, no longer owns you. What once felt like the whole of reality now appears as one layer of it.

This is the beginning of return. Not a return backward, but a return inward and then outward again. A return to the world, but from a higher octave of consciousness. A return to the body, but without the shame and confusion that once burdened it. A return to others, but without the hunger that once made you dependent on their approval, validation, or presence. A return to ordinary life, but now with sacred eyes. This is one of the great paradoxes of awakening: you do not disappear from life. You enter it more fully than before. You do not transcend the human experience by escaping it; you transcend it by becoming intimate with it without being imprisoned by it.

Awakening is not an ending. It is not a spiritual trophy. It is not a permanent mountaintop where suffering evaporates and every question is resolved. Awakening is an initiation. What comes after it is the real work: not enlightenment in the abstract, but embodiment in the ordinary. Not escape from the matrix, but a new way of walking through it. You are no longer here merely to seek truth. You are here to live from it. To hold a different vibration inside a world still entranced by fear. And this requires preparation. Because after awakening, the old architecture cannot carry the new frequency forever. Something must be released. Something must be reordered. Something must be left behind. That is why the return is sacred; it is not the descent from grace. It is the integration of it.

The Inward Collapse

Many people imagine awakening as a permanent ascent into bliss: clarity without confusion, peace without friction, light without shadow. But in reality, awakening often begins not with endless serenity, but with collapse. Not the collapse of truth, but the collapse of scaffolding. The structures that once held your identity together begin to crack. Roles that once felt essential now feel artificial. Relationships that once felt central begin to feel misaligned. Habits that once soothed you now leave an aftertaste of density. Beliefs that once gave you comfort suddenly seem hollow, too small, too inherited, too performative to contain what you now sense.

You may feel as if you are losing your life, when in truth you are losing only the life that was built around an outdated version of yourself. The false self begins to shed, and even when that shedding is holy, it can still hurt. There is grief in outgrowing who you used to be. There is sorrow in realizing that certain dreams, identities, ambitions, and attachments belonged to a consciousness you no longer inhabit. But this is not destruction; it is pruning. A tree cannot continue growing into its fuller form while carrying dead branches indefinitely. A snake cannot expand without shedding skin. What collapses is not your essence. What collapses is what can no longer house it. Many people mistake this phase for regression, thinking something is wrong because they no longer fit where they once belonged. But the collapse is not proof that awakening failed. It is proof that it is real.

Letting Go: The Art of Non-Attachment

To prepare for life after awakening, you must learn the art of letting go. This is one of the hardest teachings for the human mind, because the mind is trained to grip. It clings to certainty, to identity, to familiarity, to routine, to pain, even to suffering, if suffering at least offers a known structure. The mind fears emptiness. It fears the in-between. It fears what remains when what was once relied upon begins to dissolve. But awakening introduces a different logic. It teaches that life is not asking for your control; it is asking for your alignment. Letting go does not mean abandoning care, becoming passive, or pretending not to love what you love. It means releasing the illusion that everything must be managed, predicted, forced, or secured by personal will.

You stop chasing what has already completed its role. You stop forcing connections that belong to a prior version of yourself. You stop gripping identities that once protected you but now limit you. You release the relationship you outgrew, the role that was built around approval, the persona that was born from fear, the dream that no longer reflects your truth, the wound that became an identity, and the need to be seen in a certain way. Letting go can feel like death to the ego because the ego interprets release as loss of self. But often what you are releasing is not the self at all; it is the structure that prevented the deeper self from breathing. Letting go is not failure. It is graduation. It is the recognition that you cannot enter a new octave of being while dragging the entire architecture of your old consciousness behind you.

Letting Go as an Act of Surrender

At the heart of true release is surrender. Surrender is one of the most misunderstood words on the spiritual path: to the wounded ego, it sounds like defeat, like weakness, or resignation. But real surrender is none of these things. Surrender is not giving up. It is giving over. It is the conscious decision to trust life more than fear. To surrender is to stop living as if tension were the source of safety, to say, inwardly: I do not need to control everything to feel secure; I do not need to know every outcome before I take the next step; I do not need to grip life in order to participate in it fully; I trust that what brought me here is still carrying me. Surrender is participatory. It does not remove you from life; it harmonizes you with it.

This is why surrender feels so intimate with nature. Water does not conquer the riverbed; it moves with it. The wind does not apologize for changing direction. A tree does not resist autumn when it is time to let its leaves fall. Surrender is the return to this kind of wisdom. You stop becoming stone and become water. You stop becoming wall and become wind. And in that softening, life often begins to move with a grace that force could never produce.

Detoxing the Old

After awakening, it becomes increasingly difficult to keep consuming what once kept you numb. This is because consciousness has become more sensitive. What was once tolerated now feels heavy. What was once entertaining now feels invasive. What once seemed harmless now reveals its cost. The return therefore requires detox, not merely as a health practice, but as a spiritual realignment. Detox is the clearing of density that no longer resonates with what you are becoming. It is not punishment. It is refinement. And it happens physically, mentally, emotionally, energetically, and relationally.

Nourishing the Body

The body is no longer just something you inhabit; it becomes an instrument through which consciousness is expressed. It is your tuning fork, your vessel, your temple, your transmitter. What you consume shapes not only your chemistry, but also your clarity. Food carries vibration, memory, density, and force. Processed food, excessive sugar, chemical additives, and unconscious consumption can weigh down not only the body, but the field around it. By contrast, clean water, living foods, nourishing meals prepared with intention, and a more conscious relationship to eating begin to sharpen the inner instrument. This does not require perfection or spiritual elitism; it requires listening. It asks you to notice what leaves you clear, grounded, and alive, and what leaves you agitated, numb, or clouded. You begin eating not only for health, but for harmony, not merely to survive, but to support coherence.

Curating the Mental Diet

Attention is one of the most sacred forms of energy you possess. Where your attention goes, your nervous system follows. What you repeatedly expose yourself to becomes part of your inner atmosphere. This is why awakening often demands a drastic shift in what you consume mentally. Fear-based media, violent entertainment, outrage-driven social content, manipulative advertisements, and algorithmically amplified distraction all shape the subconscious. They program expectation, keep the body on alert, reinforce scarcity and emotional reactivity, and fragment the field. If you are trying to embody truth, but spend hours marinating in distortion, panic, envy, or noise, you are working against yourself. Choose what steadies you, what expands you, and what returns you to your own center. Your attention is your currency; spend it like it matters.

Releasing Numbness

Much of modern life is built around escape: alcohol to soften reality, caffeine to outrun exhaustion, sugar to stimulate the flattened nervous system, and constant scrolling to avoid silence. These are not moral failures; they are often attempts to regulate pain, loneliness, trauma, or internal emptiness. But after awakening, the cost of these escapes becomes more visible. What once felt like relief begins to feel like dilution. What once numbed pain now also numbs clarity. The awakened self begins to crave what makes presence deeper rather than thinner. Ceremony can replace compulsion. Mindfulness can replace sedation. Embodiment can replace dissociation. Stillness can replace the addictive search for stimulation. You begin choosing clarity over comfort, not because comfort is bad, but because truth becomes more precious than anesthesia.

Realigning Relationships and Environment

Perhaps the most painful detox after awakening happens in relationships. Some connections were built on shared wounds, mutual compensation, or unconscious agreement. They were not necessarily false, but they belonged to an earlier stage of your becoming. When you heal, those dynamics may no longer fit, not always because anyone is wrong, but because the energetic contract is changing. You may love people deeply and still no longer resonate with the version of the relationship that once held you together. But awakening often requires that you honor truth over familiarity. This is not abandonment; it is alignment. You are not required to make everyone comfortable with your evolution. Sometimes love looks like distance. Sometimes respect looks like release. Sometimes the most compassionate act is to stop pretending that misalignment is harmony.

The same is true of environment. After awakening, your surroundings matter more: your home, your workspace, your daily rhythms, the objects you keep near you, the noise you tolerate, the pace you normalize. Make your home a sanctuary. Let your routines reflect your devotion to truth. Let your environment support remembrance rather than distraction. Everything around you is teaching your nervous system what reality is. Choose carefully.

Becoming Ambivalent and Indifferent to the World

After awakening, a strange and sometimes unsettling transformation begins. Things that once seemed urgent lose their grip. Conflicts that once consumed you no longer command the same energy. Desires that once felt central begin to appear less compelling. The approval of others weakens in importance. The highs and lows of external circumstances stop owning your inner state in the same way. To the unawakened mind, this can look like numbness or withdrawal. But often it is neither; it is sovereignty. You begin to experience a kind of inner neutrality. You still feel deeply, but you are no longer enslaved by what you feel. You still care, but you do not cling. You still engage, but you do not entangle.

What once triggered you now teaches you. What once pulled you now reveals itself as passing. What once defined you now dissolves into perspective. Indifference, in its higher form, is not ignorance; it is liberation from unnecessary entanglement. It is the refusal to be owned by every passing drama. It is the capacity to let the world be what it is without collapsing into either obsession or despair. This is not deadness. It is peace.

Integration Over Escape

One of the great temptations after awakening is to want out: out of society, out of responsibility, out of ordinary life, out of the friction of human relationship, out of the systems that still seem dense, unconscious, and exhausting. But awakening does not ask you to flee the world. It asks you to stop being unconsciously shaped by it. You do not leave the matrix by physically escaping everything; you leave it inwardly by no longer letting it dictate your frequency, your worth, your center, or your consciousness. Then you return to ordinary life differently. You still pay bills. You still care for children or elders. You still face grief, illness, limitation, confusion, and change. But now you move through it differently.

You are no longer asking the world to validate your light; you carry it. You are no longer waiting for perfect conditions to embody truth; you embody it in imperfect conditions. This is how awakening becomes service: not through preaching, but through presence. It is easy to feel spiritual in isolation. It is more profound to remain luminous in traffic, in conflict, in parenting, in business, in fatigue, in uncertainty, in the repetition of daily life. This is where wisdom is tested. This is where awakening becomes real. Not in escape. In integration.

Creating from Wholeness

Before awakening, much of what people call manifestation is actually compensation. They pursue things in order to become someone: seeking success to feel worthy, love to feel complete, recognition to feel real, abundance to feel safe. But after awakening, creation begins to arise from a different place. Not lack, but wholeness. You no longer create in order to fix yourself. You create because life is moving through you. Desire becomes less desperate and more sacred. Ambition becomes less about proving and more about expressing. Purpose becomes less like obligation and more like play. Action flows not from deficiency, but from fullness. You no longer ask life to prove your worth; you become the proof of it. You no longer manifest to become someone. You create from the someone you already are. Creation stops being a strategy for self-manufacture. It becomes overflow.

Wu Wei and the Power of Effortless Action

Taoist philosophy offers a profound phrase for this state: Wu Wei, often translated as effortless action. This does not mean doing nothing, nor passivity or spiritual avoidance. It means acting in such deep alignment with reality that force becomes unnecessary. The right action arises naturally. Movement occurs without strain. Choices come with less mental violence. Life is not manipulated into submission, but entered skillfully. In Wu Wei, action flows because resistance has softened. You stop pushing every door and begin sensing which ones open. You stop trying to outsmart the river and begin learning how to move with its current.

This is one of the fruits of awakening. The nervous system becomes less frantic. The mind becomes less controlling. Intuition grows more trustworthy. Decisions arise not from panic, but from resonance. Events unfold, choices clarify, action emerges, and you move, not with passivity, but with grace. Wu Wei is what life feels like when inner conflict lessens and alignment increases. Effort does not disappear completely; it simply stops coming from strain. It comes from coherence. You become less like a swimmer thrashing against current and more like the current itself.

Responsibility Over Blame

Awakening also changes your relationship to responsibility. Before awakening, the ego survives through blame: it blames the past, the parents, the partners, the system, society, fate, God, injustice, luck, and the world. Sometimes those things have indeed caused real pain. Awakening does not require denial of that. But it does require a shift. You stop organizing your identity around who or what injured you. You begin asking a more empowering question: now that I see more clearly, what is mine to own? This is radical responsibility, not shame, not self-condemnation, but power. You begin owning your energy, your projections, your interpretations, your habits, your participation, your healing, and your contribution to the field around you.

You stop waiting for someone else to make your life whole. You stop expecting the past to become different before you permit yourself to become free. Radical responsibility is not cruel; it is liberating. Because blame keeps power outside you, while responsibility returns it. You cannot always choose what happened. But you can choose what happens through you now. That shift changes the soul.

Living as the Embodied Light

After awakening, your presence becomes your teaching. Not because you are superior or without flaw, but because there is less contradiction between what you know and how you live. Truth begins to radiate through the ordinary texture of your being. You do not have to convince anyone; you embody. You do not have to perform wisdom; you become quieter, steadier, more coherent. Your stillness says enough. This is the embodied light: not flashy, not self-important, not theatrical. It is subtle. It reveals itself in how you speak, how you listen, how you respond to difficulty, how you carry your body, how you handle silence, how you love without possession, and how you maintain integrity when no one is watching.

You become a reminder, not because you preach, but because something in your presence tells others that another way of being is possible. People feel it. They may not have language for it, but they feel the difference between someone who is still performing consciousness and someone who has begun to inhabit it. This is one of the great services of the awakened life: to become a field in which others remember themselves.

Presence: The Final Practice

After all the philosophies, purifications, collapses, releases, and realizations, what remains? Presence. Presence is the final practice because it is the ground beneath every other one. It is the homecoming at the center of awakening. It is the place where seeking softens into being. You stop waiting for special moments and begin recognizing that awareness itself makes moments holy. The dishes become practice. The traffic light becomes practice. The conversation becomes practice. The fatigue becomes practice. The laughter, the sorrow, the silence after a long cry, the stillness of dawn: all of it becomes practice. You find the sacred not only in meditation, but in the ordinary breath between tasks, in the eyes of a child, in the warmth of tea, in the mystery of simply being here at all.

Presence does not remove life's complexity; it fills it with intimacy. You stop chasing some future state where fulfillment will finally arrive. You begin to taste fulfillment in direct contact with what is.

Time slows, not literally, but energetically. One breath becomes enough. One clear moment becomes an entire world. This is not passivity; it is fullness. Presence is the place where the awakened self returns again and again until there is no difference between practice and life.

Reflection: The Returning Self

Letting go is not rejection; it is readiness. Surrender is not weakness; it is strength without aggression. Detox is not deprivation; it is refinement. Ambivalence is not withdrawal; it is inner peace. Indifference is not coldness; it is freedom from unnecessary entanglement. Presence is not mere stillness; it is fulfillment alive in the ordinary. And return is not regression. It is resurrection.

You are not who you were. And yet, in another sense, you have always been becoming this. Beneath the fear, beneath the roles, beneath the wounds and performances and long seasons of forgetting, something in you has always known the way home. Now you have remembered. You have re-entered the world not to conquer it, not to preach to it, and not to escape it, but to walk through it as a different kind of being. You are not here to force reality into your design. You are here to participate in it consciously. You are not going back. You are moving forward, awake. And from this awakened ground, a new question rises, not as pressure, but as invitation: now that you have remembered who you are, what do you choose to bring into being?

Chapter 22: The Art of Manifestation: Becoming the Living Prayer

"What you desire is not outside of you; it is already forming within the field of your awareness."

Manifestation is often misunderstood. In a world obsessed with quick fixes and instant results, the concept has been diluted into little more than wishful thinking, vision boards, and hashtags. But true manifestation is not about asking the universe for more things. It is about aligning yourself so completely with the frequency of your desired reality that it becomes inevitable. To manifest is to become the living embodiment of what you seek. It is not about convincing reality, it is about becoming reality.

The Misunderstanding of Manifestation

The popularized notion of manifestation focuses heavily on visualization, affirmations, and the Law of Attraction. While these tools can be useful, they are often applied with a limited understanding of the deeper mechanics of consciousness. You do not attract what you want. You attract what you are. The universe does not respond to begging, hoping, or fantasizing. It responds to coherence. When your thoughts, emotions, and actions align with a single frequency, reality has no choice but to reflect that back to you.

This is not magic, it is resonance.

Step One: Clarify the Signal

Everything begins with clarity. Not clarity of desire alone, but clarity of being. Many people ask for love, abundance, purpose, but their internal state is muddied with fear, doubt, and contradiction. The field responds not to your words, but to your dominant frequency. If you say, "I am ready for love," but you are vibrating with self-doubt and fear of rejection, the field will reflect confusion, not clarity.

Ask yourself: Who would I be if I already had this? Then become that. This is the first step: become the version of you who already lives in that reality.

Step Two: Emotional Alignment

Emotions are not obstacles, they are instruments. They are the tuning forks of your consciousness. Every emotion carries a frequency that either harmonizes or clashes with the reality you desire. Gratitude, joy, trust, and surrender elevate your vibration. Anxiety, neediness, and resistance distort the signal. To create in this way is to feel the outcome before you see it. To embody the joy of receiving before anything has arrived.

This is not pretending. This is activating the neural and energetic pathways that tell the quantum field: "This is my reality."

Step Three: Inspired Action

Conscious creation is not passive. It is not daydreaming on the couch. It requires movement, action aligned with intention. The universe operates through momentum. When you move, it moves with you. But the key is inspired action, not desperate action. Inspired action arises from stillness, from inner knowing. It feels light, exciting, guided. Desperate action arises from fear. Inspired action arises from alignment. Each step you take as the future version of yourself lays a foundation in the present. And that foundation magnetizes opportunities, synchronicities, and resources from the quantum field.

Step Four: Let Go of the How

The biggest saboteur of manifestation is the need to control how it will happen. The mind wants guarantees. It wants to chart the path, to control the timeline. But the field is non-linear. It works through possibilities far beyond your conscious mind. Your job is not to engineer the outcome, but to hold the vibration. Let go of the how. Let go of the when. Your only task is to remain in resonance.

Trust is the bridge between desire and fulfillment. Surrender is not giving up, it is handing over the mechanics to a greater intelligence.

Step Five: Collapse Old Timelines

Each moment offers you infinite potential paths. Each choice, thought, and feeling activates a specific timeline. When you embody your future self, you collapse all other timelines that do not match that frequency. If you continue to choose fear, doubt, or self-sabotage, you keep activating timelines that mirror those patterns. But when you choose differently, when you stop reacting to life as your past self, you sever those loops. You become the new timeline.

This is how aligned intention becomes acceleration.

The Role of Identity

The core of this entire process is identity. You do not receive what you want, you receive what matches who you believe you are. If you still see yourself as unworthy, you will unconsciously reject what you desire. Manifestation begins when you choose a new identity. Not as fantasy, but as a sacred remembrance. You are not becoming something new. You are returning to your original frequency.

Creating the Internal Environment

Just as a seed requires fertile soil, water, and sunlight, your desires require an internal environment of coherence. This means: A mind trained in focus and stillness. A heart open to receive. A nervous system that feels safe to expand. If your inner world is chaotic, what you seek to bring forth will be delayed, not as punishment, but as mercy. The field will not deliver what would overwhelm you.

This is why trauma healing is essential to this creative process. The safer you feel within yourself, the more capacity you have to hold greater realities.

Common Blocks to Manifestation

1. **Attachment to Outcome:** Wanting something so badly that your neediness becomes resistance. **Inconsistent Vibration:** Visualizing abundance in the morning, worrying about bills in the afternoon. **Unconscious Beliefs:** Childhood wounds or societal programming that say you don't deserve more. **Toxic Environment:** Surrounding yourself with low-vibrational people, media, or habits that drain your field. **Lack of Integration:** Wanting more while still living in the patterns of your old self.

All of these can be cleared, not with force, but with awareness.

Living as a Prayer

The highest form of creation is not asking; it is becoming. When your life becomes a prayer, every breath is sacred. Every step is aligned. Every moment is a mirror of your intention. You stop waiting for miracles. You start recognizing that you are the miracle. This is the art of living as a prayer: You speak as if your words are casting spells.

- You move as if grace walks with you. You love as if your heart is an altar. You create as if Source is flowing through you.

Manifestation and Service

Your desires are not random. They are encoded within your soul's blueprint. They are not just for your benefit, but for the benefit of all. When you manifest love, you radiate that love to others. When you manifest abundance, you uplift others through generosity. When you manifest clarity, you become a guide for those still lost in confusion. True manifestation is always collective. It ripples. It uplifts. It aligns with the greater harmony.

The Role of Ritual and Sacred Space

Manifestation thrives in intentional environments. Create rituals that anchor your desires: Morning affirmations. Candles lit with purpose. Journals that record your vision. Music that raises your frequency. Spaces that feel like temples. Your life is your altar. Your attention is your offering. When you walk in beauty, the universe responds.

Final Alignment: Feeling It As Done

Perhaps the most powerful shift is this: Act, feel, breathe, and think as if it is already done. Not as performance, but as truth. If you knew, with absolute certainty, that what you desired was on its way... how would you live? Live that way. That vibration will collapse time. That frequency will draw the unseen into form. This is not delusion. This is quantum alignment.

Reflection: The Living Prayer

- You do not attract what you want, you attract what you are. Your emotions are the signal. Your alignment is the language. Your identity is the magnet. To manifest is not to wish. It is to become. Surrender is not passive, it is magnetic. When your life becomes a prayer, the universe becomes a mirror. You are not waiting for your reality. Your reality is waiting for you.

Walk as if it is done. Because in the quantum field, it already is.

Manifesting from Joy: The Overflow Principle

"There is a higher octave of manifestation: one born not from need, but from the natural overflow of joy. True manifestation at this level is not born from desire, but from delight."

There comes a time in every awakening journey when struggle gives way to ease. When seeking turns to knowing. When the weight of transformation lifts, and what remains is lightness, not because life has become easier, but because you have become lighter. You have shed the illusions, purged the programming, and remembered your nature. And what rises in that remembrance is joy. Not the fleeting joy of acquisition. Not the conditioned joy of accomplishment. But the joy of being.

Joy is your natural state. It is not something to earn or chase or achieve. It is the signature of your soul's alignment with Source. It is the resonance of truth vibrating through an uncluttered vessel. And it is from this joy that the most potent manifestations arise, not out of lack, but out of overflow. In this chapter, we explore the art of manifesting not from need, but from the abundant core of your realized self. We examine the frequency of joy, the dynamics of co-creation, and the practical methods to anchor this elevated state into everyday life.

The Frequency of Joy

Joy is not a mood. It is a frequency, a state of attunement to the infinite field of possibility. When you dwell in joy, you magnetize reality to match your essence. Your outer world organizes itself around your inner harmony. In the quantum field, manifestation is less about effort and more about resonance. The field responds to what you are, not what you want. If you are anchored in lack, your desires become echoes of absence. But if you are rooted in joy, your desires become extensions of wholeness. The universe amplifies your essence.

This is why joy is so powerful. It is the evidence of alignment. It is the permission slip to receive. When you feel joyful, you are already connected to the reality your heart longs for. You are not waiting for it, you are living it, energetically. And that energy collapses timelines, accelerates synchronicity, and opens doors you never knew existed.

Need vs. Overflow

There are two frequencies from which we manifest: need and overflow. Need says, "I do not have. I must create." Overflow says, "I already am. Let it unfold." Need is rooted in survival. It is the consciousness of the wounded self, still trying to fix something, earn something, prove something. When you manifest from need, you are often chasing symbols of safety, money, status, relationships, to soothe an inner void.

But when you begin manifesting from overflow, your focus shifts. You no longer ask, "What do I need to get?" You ask, "What do I have to give?" You no longer seek fulfillment outside. You become the source of it. And the paradox is this: when you no longer need the thing, it comes to you freely. Because you are no longer blocking it with desperation. You are inviting it with joy.

Embodied Alignment: Joy in the Body

Joy is not just a mental construct. It lives in the body. You feel it in the warmth of your chest, the softness of your breath, the lightness of your step. You feel it when you laugh without reason, dance without choreography, speak without filter. To manifest from joy, you must become joy. You must let it seep into your cells, inform your posture, guide your tone. This is not performance, it is embodiment. Your body becomes a tuning fork for the frequency you wish to live.

Practices like ecstatic dance, laughter yoga, conscious movement, and somatic breathwork are powerful tools to anchor joy into your physical form. They break the loops of stagnation and open channels for authentic expression.

The Sacred Cycle of Expression

Joy naturally seeks expression. It wants to move, to speak, to create. Art, music, poetry, invention, these are not hobbies. They are manifestations of the divine impulse. They are how joy fertilizes the field of reality. When you create from joy, you are not trying to impress. You are not strategizing. You are simply overflowing. And what emerges from that overflow carries a frequency that impacts the world in unseen ways.

This is how joy becomes service. Your joy blesses others. Your radiance heals. Your laughter liberates. You do not need to preach. You only need to be full.

Conscious Choice: Honoring Joy Without Guilt

One of the final traps on the spiritual path is guilt. Guilt that you are happy when others are not. Guilt that you have abundance when others are struggling. Guilt that you no longer suffer in systems you once felt trapped by. This guilt is a remnant of the old matrix, which equates worth with suffering. But you were not born to suffer. You were born to shine.

To honor your joy is to honor the divine within you. And your joy does not diminish others, it inspires them. You give permission for others to rise when you rise without apology. You become a lighthouse by staying lit.

Joy as an Offering

True manifestation is not about what you can extract from life. It is about what you can offer. Joy is your offering. When you bring joy into your conversations, your creations, your interactions, you alter timelines. You soften defenses. You awaken hearts. You rewrite the collective dream. You do not need to solve the world's problems. You only need to walk through the world as a solution.

Joy is that solution. It doesn't ask for attention. It doesn't demand applause. It just is. Quiet. Unshakable. Contagious. When you live in joy, you become the evidence of what is possible.

The Magnetic Field of Delight

The electromagnetic field of the heart is far more powerful than the brain's. And when your heart is open and radiant, your field expands. It communicates with the quantum realm. It magnetizes experiences that match its frequency. Delight is the secret code. It is the resonance the universe responds to most quickly. So, delight in your path. Delight in your breath. Delight in the unknown.

And as you do, reality reshapes itself to delight in you.

Manifesting Without Trying

The highest form of manifestation is surrender. Not the surrender of passivity, but of presence. You do not push. You allow. You do not chase. You attract. You do not strive. You align. This is the way of Wu Wei, action through non-action. The Taoist wisdom that the river reaches the ocean not by force, but by flow. Your dreams are already moving toward you. The question is: are you open?

Joy keeps you open. Not because everything is perfect, but because you have stopped resisting what is. In that non-resistance, miracles are born.

Final Reflection

- Joy is not a reward. It is a compass. Manifestation is not forcing life to give you what you want. It is remembering that you already are what you seek. When you create from overflow, life becomes your mirror. When you live in joy, you manifest the world your soul remembers. This is the dance of joy. This is the path of the living prayer.

Not effort, but essence. Not striving, but shining. Not seeking, but singing. And now, let the music of your soul begin.

Chapter 23: The Gift of Resilience: Living Beyond Reaction

"Sometimes, in the darkness, you must become the light."

There is a moment, quiet, almost imperceptible, when the soul stops pleading with life to be gentle and begins to trust its own strength. It is not the absence of darkness that signals awakening, but the birth of a deeper light within it. Awakening is not a shield from suffering, it is the furnace that transforms it. True awakening does not erase adversity. It grants you the eyes to see through it. You begin to recognize that life will continue to move, sometimes in storms, sometimes in silence, but your relationship to its motion is what transforms everything.

You realize, perhaps for the first time, that the light you have been searching for was never outside of you. It was not in the teachings, the books, or the gurus. It was the quiet ember burning in the center of your being, waiting for you to breathe belief into it. And in that moment, you awaken to the gift of resilience, not as resistance, but as radiant surrender.

The Strength Beneath the Surface

True resilience is not the armor of invulnerability. It is the transparency of presence. It is not about denying pain, but being so fully present with it that it no longer owns you. Resilience is not forged in stillness, but in movement. It is the tree that bends with the storm yet does not break. It is the ocean that absorbs the storm and returns to calm. Resilience means knowing you will endure, not because life will be kind, but because you have become unshakeable in your truth.

You do not become resilient by numbing yourself. You become resilient by allowing yourself to feel so deeply that no feeling can uproot you. You weep and laugh. You ache and heal. You fall and rise. But you never collapse under the illusion that any of it defines you. This is how you become a living paradox: deeply open and utterly unbreakable.

The Art of Guiding Without Force

As your own awakening deepens, a desire will emerge to help others find their path. But here is the sacred challenge: you cannot awaken another through persuasion or pressure. You cannot carry them across their river of transformation. You are not a lifeboat. You are a lighthouse. A lifeboat tries to rescue, often drowning in the weight of those it carries. A lighthouse stands steady, emitting light, not to pull, but to guide. It does not run to those in peril. It remains rooted and radiant, trusting that those who are ready will navigate by its glow.

True influence comes not from arguing, but from being. Not from convincing, but from embodying. Your presence becomes the message. Your frequency becomes the invitation. You lead not with control, but with coherence. Not with urgency, but with understanding. You begin to trust that every soul is exactly where it needs to be, learning, breaking, growing in the exact ways required by its own divine curriculum. Your love no longer enables. It empowers.

Satisfaction: The Portal to Abundance

In a world addicted to striving, satisfaction is a revolutionary act. Satisfaction is not complacency, it is a shift in frequency. It is no longer seeking happiness in the future but finding it in the now. When you anchor into satisfaction, you stop creating from scarcity and begin creating from overflow. The awakened soul does not chase joy. It embodies it. It does not wait for abundance. It recognizes it.

Satisfaction allows you to access higher states of alignment. It opens the door to miracles because it signals to the universe: "I am enough. I have enough. I trust enough." From this state, manifestation becomes effortless. Not because you desire less, but because you no longer resist what is. The universe responds to gratitude with acceleration. It multiplies what you celebrate.

Ending the War Within

Resilience requires the end of resistance. The end of the internal war. You were taught to fight life, to resist death, resist failure, resist pain. But resistance does not protect. It prolongs suffering. It traps you in a loop of defending illusions. True peace comes not from victory, but from surrender. The river does not fight the rocks, it flows around them. The sun does not argue with the clouds, it shines behind them. When you stop fighting reality, you begin to dance with it.

You realize that every challenge contains an invitation to grow. Every ending hides a new beginning. Every betrayal returns you to self-trust. You begin to ask new questions: What is life trying to teach me? What part of me is ready to be seen? What outdated identity is asking to be released? Suffering becomes sacred when it births transformation. And pain becomes a compass when you stop making it an enemy.

Living As the Light

You were never meant to escape life. You were meant to illuminate it. Resilience is not gritting your teeth through hardship. It is glowing through it. It is smiling not because everything is perfect, but because you trust yourself to move through anything. Sometimes, in the darkness, you must become the light. Not because you owe the world salvation, but because you remember that you already are the light.

You do not need external conditions to be peaceful. You do not need validation to be radiant. You do not need permission to shine. Your resilience becomes your superpower. Your presence becomes your purpose. And your life becomes a living transmission of freedom.

Mental Hijacking: The Distraction Game

Yet even in awakening, the world has its traps. You may find yourself pulled into conspiracies, headlines, and narratives that seduce you with urgency and fear. Overpopulation, illegal immigration, climate catastrophes, alien invasions, political collapse, and the rise and fall of superpowers. These stories are not inherently false. But they are distractions. They pull your awareness outward into spirals of reaction. They hijack your presence. They offer the illusion of control through information.

But the truth is never in the noise. It is in the stillness. You do not awaken by decoding the latest news. You awaken by remembering your eternal nature. The awakened path is not about denying global issues, it is about disengaging from the narrative that says your salvation lies in fixing the world. The world is a mirror. Fixing your state changes the reflection.

So instead of arguing about politics, heal your trauma. Instead of fearing collapse, embody sustainability. Instead of chasing truth through headlines, anchor into the truth within you. Let others play the game. You are here to end it.

The Detox of the Old

To carry the light of awareness, you must release the weight of illusion. The matrix is not just outside of you, it's embedded in your habits, your addictions, your distractions. **Food and Water:** Your physical body is the frequency carrier for your soul. When you fill it with lifeless, processed food and polluted water, you dull your signal. Living foods vibrate at a higher frequency. Clean water is not just hydration, it is clarity. What you consume becomes what you transmit.

1. **Media and Messaging:** Every show, every headline, every post, these are not just inputs. They are programming. Violent news, sexual imagery, gossip, these imprint your subconscious. Choose content that elevates. Filter your information diet. Protect your frequency. **Addictions and Escapes:** Caffeine, alcohol, drugs, porn, compulsive scrolling, these do not just numb. They anchor. They bind your energy to lower timelines. Awakening requires presence. These habits cloud it. Release not to be pure, but to be clear.
2. **Relationships and Environments:** Your frequency determines your circle. As you rise, old connections may fall away. This is not loss. It is alignment. Honor the shift. Bless the goodbye. Create sanctuaries. Your space should reflect your soul. And remember: toxicity is not just in substances or people. It is in beliefs. You must detox the inner matrix, too, the thoughts that say you're not enough, not worthy, not ready.

Living in Truth, Regardless of the World

You are no longer here to be swayed by the world. You are here to sway it. When you embody your truth, the world adjusts. You no longer argue. You radiate. You no longer wait. You act. You no longer react. You respond. And you do this not through force, but through frequency. You become a stabilizing field in an unstable world. A soft anchor in the storm. A clear bell in the noise.

And your life begins to ripple, effortlessly, powerfully, endlessly.

Final Reflection

- Resilience is not survival, it is transcendence. You cannot awaken others by saving them; you awaken them by standing in your truth. Satisfaction is not giving up, it is giving thanks. Ending the war within is the beginning of peace without. Distractions are designed to keep you asleep, presence is your rebellion. You do not need to chase the light. You are the light. And now... you shine without apology.

Anchoring the Flame: Living the Awakening Daily

"The sacred is not a destination. It is the way you walk the path."

As this journey draws to a close, something deeper is just beginning. Not an ending, not a conclusion, but a return. The return to life as it is. The return to the present moment. The return to yourself. For many, awakening is mistaken as a peak experience, a flash of enlightenment, a singular cosmic high that defines one's spiritual success. But true awakening is not a moment. It is a movement. It is a sustained, embodied remembering that must be grounded in everyday living, or it dissipates like morning fog.

In this chapter, we will explore how to keep the flame of consciousness alive in a world that constantly tries to lull us back into slumber. Here, we anchor the esoteric into the mundane. The sacred into the simple. The infinite into the intimate. Because the real miracle is not escaping the world, but learning to remain awake within it.

The Challenge of Return

After every spiritual insight, there is a return, to the dishes, to the children, to the emails, to the aching knees and early meetings. The ego, clever and patient, waits in the mundane to reclaim its throne. But this, too, is part of the awakening. Can you stay open while driving in traffic? Can you remember your truth during an argument? Can you keep your heart soft in a world that values hardness?

These are not lesser tasks. They are the real ones. These are the temples of our training. To walk consciously in the most unconscious places, that is mastery.

Sacred Routines: Turning the Ordinary Holy

Ritual is the secret thread that binds spirit to form. Not the grand rituals of ancient temples, but the quiet ones that stitch themselves into the fabric of your day. **Lighting a candle before work** to remind yourself that your energy matters. **Blessing your food** to honor the life that sustains you. **Touching your heart** before speaking to anchor your words in truth. These small acts, done with intention, keep the channel open. They remind your cells of what you have remembered.

—

Practicing Presence in Every Act

Presence is not something you find. It is something you choose. Washing the dishes becomes a meditation on movement and texture. Walking the dog becomes communion with wind and sound. Speaking becomes a conscious offering of energy. When you live like this, everything becomes a mirror. Every act is a reflection of your state. And thus, every act becomes an opportunity to return to presence.

—

Integrating the Shadow Without Judgment

Awakening does not erase your humanness. You will still get triggered. You will still feel pain. The difference is you meet it all with new eyes. When anger arises, you ask: What is this trying to protect? When fear whispers, you respond: What have I forgotten about my power? When shame surfaces, you breathe: What would love to say to this part of me? Integration is not about perfecting yourself. It is about loving yourself completely.

—

Serving Without Sacrificing

Awakened living naturally gives rise to service. But service must not come at the cost of your own alignment. True service does not deplete. True giving does not require your suffering. To serve from fullness is a gift. To serve from emptiness is martyrdom. Your presence, when rooted and radiant, transforms more than your effort ever could.

—

Holding the Flame When Others Are Asleep

You will encounter many who are not ready to awaken. Who rejects the light. Who mock or misunderstand your clarity. You are not here to convert them. You are here to embody truth so deeply that it becomes contagious. Your stillness will speak. Your joy will ripple. Your authenticity will inspire. Be patient. Remember: once, you too were asleep. And someone, somewhere, held the light for you.

Embodying the Frequency of Your Future

The greatest teaching of this entire journey is this: **You are the creator.** And the future is not built by planning. It is sculpted by frequency. Who are you being? What are you vibrating? What do your thoughts, words, and actions align with? To anchor awakening is to live as if the future you desire is already here, not as performance, but as embodiment. This is how reality bends. This is how timelines shift. This is how the dream changes.

Gratitude: The Perpetual Portal

Nothing opens the heart like gratitude. Not the kind that comes after receiving. But the kind that precedes it. Gratitude as a state of being is the most magnetic frequency of all. It says: I trust. It says: I see the gift even in this. It says: I am not waiting to love my life. I love it now.

You Are the Flame

All that you have remembered, about consciousness, creation, frequency, reality, emotion, vibration, soul contracts, karmic loops, awakening, surrender, and presence, must now return to one place: **You.** You are not a seeker anymore. You are the answer you were looking for. You are not trying to become enlightened. You are learning how to remain who you truly are. You are not here to float above life. You are here to embody divinity in every gesture. In every thought. In every choice.

Your flame is eternal. Your light is needed. Walk gently now. Walk bravely. Walk fully. **You are awake.**

Chapter 24: The Temple Within: Reclaiming the Sacred Body

"Your body is not a cage. It is a cathedral."

For many on the spiritual path, the body has been viewed as a limitation, a flawed vessel to be transcended, a distraction from higher realms. This misperception has been inherited from centuries of dogma that equated spirituality with denial, purity with punishment, and divinity with disembodiment. But what if the body is not an obstacle to awakening, but the gateway? This chapter is a reclamation. A return. A re-consecration of the sacred space you inhabit. It is a remembering that your body is not something you possess. It is something you are. And through it, the infinite gets to dance in form.

The Body as the Living Temple

The ancient mystics understood that the body is a temple, a sacred site of divine experience. Every breath is a chant. Every heartbeat a drum. Every cell a congregation of light. To reject the body is to reject the very tool through which presence is made real. In this human experience, spirit did not descend into matter as a punishment. It did so as an act of love. Your incarnation is not a fall. It is a gift. The body is the altar upon which your awareness makes offerings of experience. Pleasure, pain, sensation, silence, all are sacred. All are holy.

To reclaim your body as sacred is to begin treating it with reverence. It is to listen. To feel. To honor. It is to turn away from shame and move into intimacy, with breath, with movement, with sensation. Your flesh is not a prison. It is presence embodied.

Healing the War Within

Many carry wounds not just in the heart or mind, but in the flesh. Trauma lives in the body. It nests in the nervous system, in the muscles, in the posture, in the breath. The body remembers what the mind forgets. And often, it carries the burden of rejection, from yourself. To reclaim the sacred body, one must first end the war against it. This means forgiving your body for being human. For aging. For feeling. For changing. It means no longer speaking to it with contempt or forcing it to conform to false ideals of beauty or strength.

When you release the need to control the body, you create space to commune with it. This is not about perfection. This is about presence. You learn to ask: What do you need? How do you feel? What are you trying to say? The healing begins not when the pain disappears, but when you learn to sit with it. To breathe with it. To honor it as a teacher, not a tyrant.

Embodiment as Spiritual Practice

True spirituality is not about leaving the body. It is about fully arriving in it. Embodiment is not the opposite of transcendence, it is the fulfillment of it. Embodiment means showing up. It means being here, fully, with all of your senses awake and alive. It is the experience of drinking tea with reverence. Of walking barefoot on the earth with gratitude. Of dancing without needing to look graceful. Of making love as a form of prayer.

In embodiment, your body becomes an instrument of awareness. A compass for truth. A tuning fork for intuition. Your gut knows. Your skin feels. Your heart speaks. You do not need to ascend to find the divine. You need only descend, into your own form.

The Sacred Rhythms of the Body

The body has its own wisdom, its own language, its own rhythms. It speaks in pulses and sensations, in aches and intuitions. When you ignore these messages, dis-ease arises. When you listen, alignment returns. Modern life has taught us to override the body, to ignore hunger, suppress fatigue, push past pain. But to live spiritually is to return to harmony with these natural rhythms. Sleep becomes sacred. Nourishment becomes intuitive. Rest becomes a form of worship.

You begin to live not by clocks, but by cycles. Not by obligation, but by resonance. You honor the ebb and flow of your energy, the rise and fall of your breath, the expansion and contraction of your emotions. The moon pulls your tides. The seasons shape your moods. You are not separate from nature. You are nature, made conscious.

Sexual Energy: The Fire of Creation

One of the most misunderstood aspects of the sacred body is its sexual energy. Often suppressed or distorted, this life force is the very energy of creation. It is not inherently lustful or profane. It is divine. It is the fire that births worlds. To reclaim your sexual energy is not to indulge it unconsciously, but to harness it consciously. It is to move beyond shame and into sovereignty. To recognize that your desire is not dirty. It is sacred. It is the call of life to express itself through you.

When sexual energy is cultivated with awareness, it becomes creative fuel. It can be channeled into art, into healing, into manifestation. Tantra, for example, teaches that when sexual energy rises without being released, it awakens higher centers of consciousness. This is not repression. It is redirection. It is learning to work with the fire, not extinguish it.

Movement as Medicine

The body is made to move. Stagnation is not just physical, it is energetic. When we move with intention, we unlock trapped emotions, restore vitality, and reconnect with the divine intelligence within. Movement is prayer in action. Whether it's dance, yoga, walking, or simply stretching with awareness, each gesture becomes a celebration of life. You begin to move not to perform, but to feel. You shake to release grief. You sway to feel joy. You stretch to awaken stillness. Movement becomes a language through which the soul speaks.

The Breath as the Bridge

If the body is the temple, then the breath is the holy spirit moving through it. Breath is the bridge between the seen and unseen, the conscious and subconscious. Every breath you take is a reminder that life is flowing through you. Breathwork practices help unlock stored trauma, activate inner stillness, and deepen your connection to Source. With each inhale, you draw in presence. With each exhale, you release the past.

You no longer take breathing for granted. You turn it into ritual. Into remembrance.

Nourishment as Sacred Communion

Food is not fuel. It is communion. The act of eating becomes an opportunity to honor the earth, to honor your body, to honor the sacred exchange of life. You begin to choose food not just for taste or convenience, but for vibration. Fresh, living foods carry light. They carry intelligence. When you eat in gratitude, you absorb not just nutrients, but presence. Digestion becomes an alchemical process, the transformation of earth into consciousness.

Fasting, when approached with intention, becomes not deprivation but devotion. A clearing of space. A return to simplicity. A sacred pause.

Body Image and Divine Reflection

We are conditioned to judge our bodies through the lens of comparison and critique. But your body is not a product. It is a process. It is not meant to be perfect. It is meant to be yours. Every scar, every wrinkle, every curve and line tells a story. They are not flaws. They are prayers written in flesh. When you learn to see your body as sacred, you stop measuring it by external standards. You begin to see it as a divine work of art.

Your body is not separate from your spiritual path. It is your spiritual path.

Reclaiming the Sacred Body

To reclaim the sacred body is to live from within it. To listen to its wisdom. To honor its needs. To celebrate its uniqueness. It is to stop waiting for it to be different and start loving it as it is. This is not a one-time awakening. It is a practice. A relationship. A remembering. You begin to trust your body. You begin to thank your body. You begin to feel, fully and without shame.

And as you do, you realize: You are not a soul trapped in a body. You are a soul dancing as a body. You are not here to escape your form. You are here to illuminate it. You are not here to punish your body. You are here to praise it. You are the temple. You are the priest. You are the prayer. And your sacred body is the altar upon which love is made real.

Chapter 25: The Embodied Path: Living as the Bridge Between Worlds

"You are not the light because you shine above others. You are the light because you remember you were born of it, and now walk it into form." There comes a time after the awakening, after the deconstruction, after the dark night and the rising light, when a new chapter begins. It is not marked by fireworks or profound downloads from the heavens, but by the humblest of acts: waking up and choosing to live with your awareness fully embodied.

This is the chapter of return. But it is not a return to the past or a former identity. It is a return to earth, with your soul intact. It is where the spiritual meets the practical. Where divine remembrance is no longer reserved for mountaintops or meditative highs, but where it is brought home into daily life, into your body, into your community, and into your choices. This is the embodied path.

Becoming the Bridge

Many ancient traditions speak of the rainbow bridge, the arc between heaven and earth, between divinity and mortality, between the formless and the formed. The awakened human is that bridge. Not because they reject the material world, but because they have learned how to carry the divine through it. To walk the embodied path is to no longer separate the sacred from the secular. You do not switch off your divinity when entering a grocery store, a traffic jam, or a board meeting. You carry it in every glance, in every word, in every silence. You become a portal between dimensions. You are here to walk the worlds, not just astrally or symbolically, but literally.

This chapter of life becomes less about escaping the illusion and more about participating in it with clarity. You no longer run from density, you walk through it with light. You no longer fight the matrix, you alchemize it by your presence. You become the living integration of your higher knowing and your human vessel.

The Temple of the Body

For too long, the spiritual path was seen as a detachment from the body. We were taught that the flesh is flawed, the earth is corrupt, and desire is dangerous. But this old paradigm collapses as you embody your truth. The body is not a barrier to divinity. It is its vessel. You learn to listen to the intelligence of your cells, to follow the wisdom of your gut, to honor the temple of your form. You nourish yourself not just for health, but for alignment. Movement becomes prayer. Stillness becomes presence. Your breath, your heartbeat, your sexuality, all of it becomes sacred ground.

You understand that you are not just spirit having a human experience. You are spirit expressing itself through human design. The body is the bridge, not the burden. And so, you care for it with reverence. Not out of fear or vanity, but out of devotion. You become attuned to what energizes or drains you, to what enlivens or contracts you. You choose environments, relationships, and habits that harmonize with your frequency. You let go of that which pollutes your vessel.

This embodiment is not perfection. It is presence. It is not about becoming flawless, but becoming whole.

Sacred Service and Purpose

When you embody your path, your life becomes service, not service as sacrifice, but service as overflow. You do not need to preach, convert, or save. You become the message by how you live. Your purpose becomes less about a singular mission and more about being an open channel. Some days that looks like creating art. Other days it looks like washing dishes with presence. You begin to see that there is no hierarchy of sacredness. Every moment is holy.

You serve by listening deeply. You serve by seeing clearly. You serve by creating beauty. You serve by telling the truth. You serve by showing up. You may be called into leadership, healing, teaching, or parenting. You may be called into activism, entrepreneurship, or retreat. It does not matter the outer role, what matters is the consciousness you bring to it. You become a tuning fork for truth. A mirror for awakening. A presence of integrity. And in this, your life becomes your greatest offering.

Navigating the Human Messiness

Embodiment is not utopia. It is not a bypass of life's messiness. In fact, it requires greater courage, for now you feel everything more deeply. You can no longer numb or pretend. You grieve more fully. You celebrate more tenderly. You meet your triggers as teachers. You face conflict with compassion. You hold boundaries without guilt. You cry without shame. You laugh without holding back.

You stop avoiding the human experience, and instead become more fully present within it. This presence is your power. It doesn't mean you never fall, it means you fall consciously. And you rise with more wisdom each time. You no longer need to have it all figured out. You embrace the mystery. You allow the unknown. You soften into the unfolding.

Living the Light Subtly

The world may not notice your transformation. There may be no parade, no applause, no viral post celebrating your embodiment. And that's okay. You are not here for validation. You are here to embody truth. The path of the embodied one is subtle. You change the world not by shaking it violently, but by holding it gently. You shift timelines by smiling with sincerity. You awaken others not with speeches, but with stillness.

You walk lightly. You speak kindly. You act deliberately. You do not need to announce your awakening. Your presence announces it for you.

The Ordinary Becomes Holy

The deeper you walk this path, the more the ordinary becomes extraordinary. You see the divine in the eyes of a stranger. You taste the sacred in a simple meal. You hear guidance in the rustle of leaves. You feel connection in the silence between words. You no longer seek magic, you see it everywhere. And so, your life becomes less about chasing moments of bliss and more about being deeply rooted in whatever arises. You let your enlightenment be tested in traffic, in heartbreak, in taxes, in parenting, in aging.

You bring the light into the mundane. And in doing so, you realize that nothing was ever mundane.

The Path That Never Ends

Embodiment is not a finish line. It is not a certificate or a title. It is a continual deepening. There will be cycles. Seasons. Moments of forgetting and moments of remembering. There will be days when the matrix feels loud again, when the ego gets triggered, when the body feels heavy. And this too is sacred. You meet yourself in each moment with love. You do not shame the backslide. You do not idolize the peak. You understand that the spiral of growth is infinite.

You keep showing up. You keep softening. You keep choosing presence. And in this, you discover something rare: Peace. Not the peace of escape. But the peace of participation. Not the peace of having no pain. But the peace of no longer resisting it. Not the peace of perfection. But the peace of wholeness.

Reflection: Walking the Bridge

- You are the bridge between spirit and matter, and your body is the living temple. Embodiment is not about escaping the world, but about entering it more fully, more truthfully, and more lovingly. Every act becomes sacred when done with presence. You change the world not through force, but through frequency. The light you carry is not in your words, but in your walk. Your embodiment is the gift. Your presence is the prayer. Your life is the altar.

And now, you walk the path not only awakened, but alive.

Chapter 26: The Collective Pulse: Awakening the Heart of Humanity

"You are not alone in your awakening. The Earth itself is remembering."

As the individual awakens from the illusion, a greater truth stirs beneath the surface of the world: humanity, too, is waking up. Not in unison, not in perfect harmony, but in rhythm. In pulses. In waves. Each soul that heals, each mind that remembers, sends a signal into the collective field. And slowly, that field begins to vibrate at a higher frequency. This chapter explores the transformation of not just the individual, but the collective. It traces the pulse of a civilization in metamorphosis, and it reminds the reader: what you do in your heart affects the entire human dream.

The Morphogenetic Field and Shared Consciousness

Rupert Sheldrake proposed that there exists a morphogenetic field, a blueprint of collective memory and behavior that influences not just individual organisms, but entire species. Every choice you make, every fear you release, every act of love you embody, adds to the field. It shifts the probability for others to do the same. You do not live in isolation. Your consciousness is wired into a network that spans the globe. The insights you receive, the lessons you integrate, the frequencies you emit, these ripple outward and subtly encourage similar awakenings in others.

Like tuning forks, we begin to vibrate in coherence. One healed soul inspires another. One awakened heart becomes a lighthouse. Your inner transformation is not private. It is planetary.

The Earth's Response: Schumann Resonance and Solar Shifts

The Earth, too, is not passive. She is a sentient being, holding her own frequency: the Schumann resonance. Over the past decades, that frequency has begun to spike, mirror, and respond to the rising consciousness of her inhabitants. Some call this the quickening. Others refer to it as the Great Shift. Regardless of name, the evidence is experiential: time feels distorted, synchronicities increase, intuitive abilities expand, and dense emotions surface to be transmuted.

Solar flares, electromagnetic disruptions, increased global unrest, these are not mere physical phenomena. They are energetic reflections of a species undergoing rapid spiritual evolution. As above, so below. As within, so without.

The Role of the Lightworker and the Empath

In this shifting field, some individuals carry codes. You may be one of them. You feel deeply, often unbearably so. You sense emotions before they're spoken. You intuit truths others are still resisting. You may feel like a misfit, a wanderer, or someone who never truly belonged. But in truth, you are here on purpose. You are a stabilizer. A transmitter. A way-shower. Your job is not to save the world. It is to embody a new way of being. To anchor love in places filled with fear. To hold the vision of a new earth when others still cling to the old.

This mission is not one of force. It is one of frequency. When you choose peace, others feel it. When you choose authenticity, others find courage. When you choose to heal, you give silent permission for others to do the same. This is sacred work. Invisible, but not unnoticed. The field remembers.

Breakdown Before Breakthrough

Humanity stands at a precipice. And like any transformation, there is a contraction before the expansion. We see it in the collapse of old institutions, the exposure of corruption, the polarization of perspectives. We feel it in the collective anxiety, the fragmentation of truth, the yearning for meaning. These are not signs of doom. They are signs of detox. The old paradigm, built on control, separation, scarcity, and fear, must crumble. It must be seen clearly to be released. And this process is not neat. It is messy. Emotional. Raw.

But it is also divine. Every collapsed illusion creates space for a deeper truth. Every broken system invites a reimagining. Every crumbling tower reveals the sky behind it.

From Fear to Freedom

The greatest prison of the old world was fear: fear of failure, fear of rejection, fear of death, fear of not being enough. These fears kept humanity small, docile, easily manipulated. But the new paradigm is born of freedom. Not the chaotic freedom of unchecked ego, but the sovereign freedom of the awakened soul. This freedom does not fight the system, it transcends it. It refuses to obey unconscious scripts. It rewrites reality from the inside out.

And this freedom is contagious. As more individuals remember their true nature, as more beings choose love over fear, the collective field recalibrates. New systems emerge. New stories take root. New civilizations begin to dream themselves into form.

Humanity in Chrysalis

Right now, humanity is a caterpillar dissolving in the cocoon. The old identity is disintegrating. The new form is not yet known. This in-between is uncomfortable. The world feels unrecognizable. And yet, within the chaos, new wings are forming. You are part of this metamorphosis. Your clarity is the DNA of tomorrow's society. Your courage to question, to feel, to trust, seeds the collective heart.

You are not here to fix the old. You are here to embody the new.

Signs of Collective Awakening

Despite what the news might say, awakening is accelerating. You see it in the eyes of strangers. You hear it in the language of youth. You feel it in the increased compassion during global events. Mass meditations influencing measurable global outcomes Increased reports of synchronicity and intuitive insight A surge in holistic healing, plant medicine, and energy work Movements toward decentralized systems, regenerative agriculture, and conscious entrepreneurship

These are not trends. They are birth pangs of a new earth.

The Heart of Humanity

At the core of this evolution lies the heart. Not romantic love, not performative kindness, but embodied, unconditional presence. A love that does not seek to own. A compassion that includes the self. A unity that recognizes diversity not as a threat, but as divine design. When enough hearts open, the collective mind heals. When enough beings choose truth, the collective illusion dissolves. When enough souls awaken, the dream changes.

And it begins with you.

The Dream Is Changing

The dream is not ending. It is evolving. We are not here to escape Earth. We are here to sanctify it. We are not here to transcend humanity. We are here to become fully human, in the most divine sense of the word. You are not separate from the collective. You are its cell, its breath, its voice. Every time you forgive, you cleanse the bloodline. Every time you choose peace; you heal a war that could have erupted. Every time you love without condition, you raise the ceiling of what is possible for this species.

This is the work now. This is the call. To awaken not just for the self, but for the all. To become a living signal of coherence, courage, and compassion. To pulse so brightly with presence that the entire collective field begins to remember its light. **Reflection** The Earth is not merely reacting to us; she is evolving with us. Collective awakening begins with individual alignment.

- You are not here to save the world. You are here to embody what the world is becoming. One awakened heart has the power to influence thousands. You are not alone in your light. You are part of a rising tide. And now, as the dream continues, you remember: The dreamer is no longer sleeping. The dream itself is shifting. And you are both witness and weaver of the new world to come.

Chapter 27: The Architects of Meaning: Becoming a Conscious Reality Designer

"You are not simply here to observe reality. You are here to shape it."

We have traveled far in this book, from the illusion of form to the awakening of the dreamer, through the mechanics of the matrix and the emergence of divine sovereignty. Each chapter has peeled back a layer of the simulation, revealing both the illusion and the light beneath it. But now, we arrive at a new kind of responsibility, a sacred power born not from conquest, but from clarity. The power to become a conscious architect of reality.

This chapter is not just an exploration of philosophy or mysticism, it is a blueprint. A manual for becoming the kind of being who no longer stumbles through life reacting, but who consciously chooses the narrative, vibration, and direction of their existence. This is not the end of the awakening, it is the beginning of applied mastery.

The Shift from Seeker to Creator

For much of the human journey, we live as seekers, searching for meaning, truth, peace, and purpose. We look outward, hoping the world will show us who we are and why we are here. But the path of the conscious architect begins the moment we realize that the meaning we seek is not hidden out there, it is born from within. The architect does not seek signs. They create them. The architect does not beg for clarity. They declare it. The architect does not plead with life. They shape it.

And to do so, they must embody a critical realization: reality is malleable. It responds not to effort, but to alignment. Not to willpower, but to resonance. This is the turning point where your internal state becomes your compass, and your reality begins to mirror your mastery.

Setting the Foundation: Intention Over Impulse

The first tool of the conscious reality designer is **intention**. Not a passing wish or vague hope, but a deliberate, felt, emotionally-charged decision that sets the tone for what is to come. Every morning becomes a ritual. Every thought becomes a choice. Every word becomes a spell. Intentions are the architecture of reality. They form the scaffolding upon which manifestation takes shape. Unlike goals, which are often mental and linear, intentions are vibrational and multidimensional. They influence not just outcomes, but the quality of the journey.

Ask yourself: What energy do I choose to embody today? What feeling do I wish to live in? What version of myself am I committed to expressing? These questions are not philosophical, they are practical. Because the moment you set a clear intention, your field begins to reorganize around it.

Emotions as Navigational Tools

As explored earlier in this journey, your emotions are not obstacles, they are information. They are not to be suppressed, but listened to. In this phase of your awakening, emotions become your **guidance system**. Joy, peace, curiosity, these are signs you are in alignment. Resentment, guilt, fear, these are signals of misalignment. The architect does not shame their emotions. They use them. They feel without drowning. They learn without looping. Every emotional wave is a message from the deeper field of consciousness.

When emotions are integrated, they become fuel. Passion drives purpose. Grief deepens compassion. Anger activates boundaries. The key is not to be emotionless, but to become **emotionally intelligent**, using feelings as energetic coordinates to chart your course.

The Power of Decision and Non-Attachment

One of the paradoxes of creation is this: to receive fully, you must release completely. This is where **letting go** becomes a cornerstone of conscious design. As stated in Chapter 21, letting go is not failure. It is freedom. It is surrender, not to chaos, but to flow. When you cling, you distort. When you chase, you delay. When you fear, you block. Letting go is the clearing of the canvas. It is the act of non-attachment that says: "I trust that what I desire is either arriving, or being replaced by something even better."

Letting go is not passive. It is deeply intentional. It is **making space** for the new. It is the sacred discipline of surrender, where you stop trying to force timelines and begin to **flow with precision**.

The Embrace of the Ego

To design reality, you must understand the **role of the ego**. Not as an enemy, but as a tool. The ego is the interface through which the soul navigates density. It is your avatar. Your operating system. When wounded, it creates distortion. When healed, it becomes a servant of the soul. In an earlier chapter, we explored the illusions of identity. Now, we return to integrate them. You must learn to **love the ego without becoming it**. It is not your master. It is your mirror. It shows you where you are holding separation, and gives you the chance to return to wholeness.

You do not destroy the ego to awaken. You educate it. You soothe it. You reprogram it to serve the truth rather than the trauma. This is integration. And integrated beings create integrated worlds.

Learning from the Past Without Repeating It

Every pattern you've lived has been a teacher. But the architect does not loop in memory. They harvest the wisdom and move forward. They **mine the gold from the pain** and use it to construct new paradigms. Forgiveness becomes a technology. Not to justify wrongs, but to untether from them. To forgive is to release energetic debt. It is not a moral act, it is a vibrational one. It is reclaiming your frequency from the grip of the past.

When you forgive, you reclaim energy. When you integrate, you unlock clarity. When you bless your past, you empower your future.

Discernment of Inputs

You are a filter. A receiver. A vibrational processor of the world. To live as an architect, you must be **ruthless in your discernment**: What you eat fuels your frequency. What you consume mentally programs your perception. What you tolerate determines your trajectory. As discussed in Chapter 21, the detox of the old is not punishment, it is preparation. Your energy is precious. Your attention is currency. Spend it wisely. Invest it in what aligns with your vision, not your distraction.

This includes current world narratives. As mentioned in Chapter 23, falling too deeply into conspiracies, overpopulation, alien fear, wars, climate catastrophes, can hijack your bandwidth. They may contain truth, but they are also traps. If they pull you into fear, they lower your frequency. You must rise **above the noise** to access the signal.

Power vs Force: The Wu Wei Principle

David Hawkins' book *Power vs. Force* outlines a critical truth: true power does not need to dominate. It does not require force. It is magnetic, not coercive. This wisdom echoes the Taoist principle of **Wu Wei**, effortless action. When you are in alignment, your actions require **less force but create greater impact**. You no longer push reality, you pull it. You radiate. You attract. This is the art of **doing without doing**. Of moving with the current. Of making choices not from panic, but from presence. It is the dance of co-creation.

Collapsing Timelines Through Conscious Choice

Every choice you make is a fork in the road. Every decision collapses probabilities. When you become intentional, you are no longer wandering through timelines, you are designing them. You become a **quantum sculptor**, collapsing realities into form through clarity, emotion, belief, and action. You stop fearing the future and start selecting it. And in this field of infinite potentials, you anchor the one that matches your **signature frequency**.

Becoming Ambivalent, Indifferent, and Present

To design reality, you must detach from needing any particular outcome to happen a certain way. This is not apathy, it is **sovereign neutrality**. Ambivalence allows you to be unmoved by the opinions of others. Indifference frees you from the emotional hooks of outcomes. Presence keeps you rooted in now, where all power resides. You are not cold. You are clear. You are not passive. You are poised.

And from that grounded presence, you become a powerful transmitter, a beacon that shapes reality not through reactivity, but through resonance.

Presence: The Master Key

Presence is the master frequency. It is the purest portal to creation. When you are fully present, you are fully powerful. You are not fractured into regrets or projections. You are **here, now, aligned**. From presence, you: Hear your intuition without distortion. Make decisions without fear. Act without hesitation. Create without ego. Presence is not passive. It is potent. It is the state in which your words become spells, your actions become rituals, and your very breath becomes a declaration of alignment.

Final Reflection

You are no longer lost in the illusion. You are no longer bound by the script. You are the architect now. The dreamer awakes. The creator remembering. This chapter is your blueprint: Set your intentions. Trust your emotions. Release control. Forgive the past. Discern your inputs. Flow with precision. Collapse timelines through choice. Stand in presence. This is the sacred art of conscious reality design. This is how you remember who you truly are:

Not a product of circumstance. But a sculptor of worlds. A transmitter of frequency. A weaver of dreams. And now, you begin again, not as a seeker. But as an architect of meaning itself.

Chapter 28: The Map Forward: Living as the Creator

"You are not here to find the path. You are here to become it."

Awakening is not the end of the journey. It is the beginning of a conscious life. The moment you remember your nature as awareness, your reality becomes a canvas, not something you survive, but something you shape. The world you experience is no longer a fixed destination; it becomes a mirror, a fluid field of possibility responding to your choices, beliefs, and energetic state. This chapter is your map, a compass to navigate the post-awakening terrain with intention, presence, and creative power.

The Power of Intention

Everything begins with intention. Intention is not just a wish or desire, it is the energetic blueprint of manifestation. It is the frequency you emit that organizes and shapes reality around you. Most people drift through life with reactive thoughts and inherited goals. But when you awaken, you recognize that every moment is a seed. Every thought plants a possibility. You no longer act from habit; you act from awareness.

Set intentions not only for what you want to experience, but for how you wish to *be*. Choose peace. Choose clarity. Choose authenticity. These intentions are not rigid goals; they are directions of alignment. When your being and your doing merge, you begin to move through the world with coherence, and life responds in kind.

Emotional Alignment: The Language of Reality

Emotion is the energetic language of the universe. It is not just a personal experience, it is a vibrational signal that magnetizes reality. When your emotions are in alignment with your intentions, manifestation accelerates. But emotional mastery is not about suppressing negativity. It is about presence with what arises. Anger, sadness, fear, they are not wrong. They are messengers. Honor them. Listen. Feel them fully. And then release them with love.

Return to elevated states not by force, but by choice. Gratitude. Joy. Curiosity. These are frequencies that open doors. They align you with timelines where your soul flourishes.

Lessons from the Past: Your Story as Medicine

Every moment of your life has been part of your awakening. There are no wasted experiences. Even the pain, even the failures, especially the failures, contain seeds of wisdom. To move forward, you must be willing to look back, not to dwell, but to learn. The past is not a prison. It is a teacher. Revisit your story with new eyes. What patterns kept repeating? What beliefs drove your decisions? What traumas shaped your perception?

When you witness your past without judgment, you transmute it. You free yourself from the cycle. You stop being the character and become the author. This is how karma resolves, not through punishment, but through realization.

Responsibility as Empowerment

Taking full responsibility for your life is not blame, it is liberation. It is the recognition that nothing outside of you determines your destiny. Your perception, your choices, your vibration, these are your true levers of creation. Responsibility is not a burden. It is sovereignty. It is the sacred acknowledgment that you are no longer a pawn in someone else's game. You are the dreamer.

And as the dreamer, you must choose with care. Your thoughts are not idle. Your energy is not inconsequential. Every moment is creative.

Forgiveness as Energetic Liberation

To create freely, you must release the chains of resentment. Forgiveness is not for the other person. It is for your alignment. It is the unblocking of your energy. Holding onto blame, anger, or guilt keeps you tethered to old timelines. It ties up your life force in the past. But when you forgive, you reclaim that energy. You become whole again. Forgive not because they deserve it, but because you deserve peace. Forgive yourself not because you never erred, but because you are no longer that version of you. You have evolved. Let the past version of you go, with love.

The Detox of the Old

To carry the light of awareness, we must release the weight of illusion. The matrix is not just outside of us, it is encoded in our habits, our addictions, our distractions. To rise into resonance with what is true, we must leave behind what no longer serves. **Food and Water:** What we consume becomes part of us, not just physically, but energetically. Processed food, chemical additives, synthetic ingredients, and polluted water cloud the vessel through which consciousness expresses itself. A living body needs living food, fruits, vegetables, seeds, herbs, clean water, and sunlight. Food prepared with intention becomes medicine. Water blessed with gratitude becomes a conduit for clarity.

1. **Media and Messaging:** Information is vibrational. News, entertainment, social media, these shape perception. Fear, division, gossip, violence, these are toxins of the mind. Choose content that inspires, uplifts, expands. Protect your mental diet as fiercely as your physical one. **Addictions and Escapes:** Unconscious consumption of substances, stimulation, or distraction weakens your signal. Alcohol, drugs, pornography, endless scrolling, these are not just habits. They are energetic chains. Letting go is not repression, it is refinement. When your light grows, you can no longer tolerate what dims you.

2. **Relationships and Environments:** As you ascend, your resonance changes. Some relationships will feel misaligned. That's not failure, it's evolution. Let go with grace. Create environments that support your peace. Clutter, chaos, and noise hinder expansion. Curate your space as you would your mind. And beneath all of this is a deeper truth: much of what we label as "toxic" is not inherently evil. It is simply the result of unconscious agreement. When you begin to question your beliefs, about food, media, behavior, and even suffering, you

start to see clearly. Toxicity is often a mirror, reflecting where we have yet to become aware.

Letting Go: The Art of Non-Attachment

Letting go is not about defeat. It is about trust. It is an act of sacred surrender, not of willpower, but of alignment. When you stop chasing, when you stop clinging, life begins to breathe with you. Letting go is not a denial of desire, it is the release of *need*. You set your intention, you align your energy, and then... you let the universe deliver.

Letting go is an act of *surrender*. To surrender is not to give up. It is to open up. It is to release control, knowing that a higher intelligence is orchestrating all things. It is the ego stepping aside so that the soul can lead. Surrender does not mean passive inaction. It means no longer resisting the flow. It is trusting the timing. Trusting the unfolding. Trusting that what is yours will find you.

You do not cling to what is aligned. You do not fear what is real. You simply allow.

Wu Wei and the Power of Flow

In Taoist philosophy, the principle of **Wu Wei** describes effortless action, flowing with the current of life rather than against it. When we stop trying to control, force, or over-effort our way forward, we begin to act from alignment rather than resistance. You don't need to hustle your way into your highest reality. You simply align with it. You become it. And from that place of energetic coherence, right action arises naturally.

Life moves through you, not because you manipulate it, but because you've become a vessel through which truth can move.

Power vs Force: The Energetics of Decision

As Dr. David Hawkins wrote in his groundbreaking work "Power vs Force," true power is effortless. It emanates from coherence, integrity, and clarity. Force is brittle, temporary, and fear-based. When you make decisions from fear, desperation, or ego, you are using force. When you choose from inner knowing, calm confidence, and deep resonance, you are accessing power. Every choice becomes a tuning fork. Are you vibrating with truth? Or reacting from scarcity?

True manifestation does not happen through striving, it happens through being. When you align with your highest truth, all that is meant for you begins to unfold.

Collapsing Alternate Timelines

In the quantum field, every possibility already exists. Your choices are not creating reality from nothing, they are selecting from infinite timelines. When you choose love over fear, truth over illusion, authenticity over performance, you collapse one version of reality and step into another. Each choice is a ripple that rewrites the code. This is not theory. This is how you live as a quantum being.

You are no longer bound to your past. You are not destined to repeat your wounds. You are a living interface with the multiverse.

Ambivalence, Indifference, and Presence

A curious aspect of mastery is *ambivalence*. Not in the sense of apathy, but in the sense of detachment from outcome. You no longer need reality to go a certain way. You simply *are*, and life flows around that beingness. *Indifference* is not coldness. It is freedom. It is the end of obsession. It is the spaciousness that allows life to surprise you. And *presence* is the ultimate power. In presence, all timelines collapse. The past has no pull. The future has no urgency. Only this moment exists, and this moment contains everything.

Presence is where miracles are born. When you are fully here, you are already there.

Final Reflection

You are not here to fix the world. You are here to remember who you are. Life does not respond to effort, it responds to resonance. The map is not outside of you. It is encoded in your frequency. You are not here to escape the matrix. You are here to outgrow it. The game has changed. You are no longer the seeker. You are the signal.

Live accordingly.

Chapter 29: Techniques and Methods for Raising and Aligning Your Vibration

"In Chapter 22, we explored the philosophy of conscious manifestation: how creation flows from wholeness rather than lack, and how alignment matters more than effort. These 14 practices that follow are not separate from that philosophy. They are its activation. The energy you embody determines the reality you experience."

In the grand tapestry of awakening, realization is only the beginning. To live the truth you have uncovered, you must become the vibration of that truth. Conscious manifestation does not occur through wishful thinking or intellectual understanding alone. It happens through alignment. **Alignment** is the resonance between your inner state and the outer reality you wish to embody. If the earlier chapters have been a map of the dream's structure, how it is formed, forgotten, and remembered, this chapter is your toolkit. Here we explore the *practical* methods by which you raise your frequency, entrain your mind to higher truths, and become a living conduit for the divine intelligence that pulses through all things.

Conscious creation is not magic. It is **resonance**. And to resonate with your ideal timeline, you must first elevate the internal vibration that attracts it.

---

1. Meditation: The Foundation of Inner Alignment

Meditation is not just a relaxation technique; it is vibrational attunement. When you sit in stillness, you are not trying to escape the world, you are returning to the field of pure awareness that creates it. **Mindfulness Meditation** trains you to observe your thoughts as they arise, creating distance between identity and narrative. This dissolves emotional reactivity and increases coherence in the mind. **Guided Visualization** takes you on an inner journey, often into a future self or reality. These visual maps can be powerful tools for programming the subconscious and generating emotional resonance with your desires.

- **Transcendental Meditation**, using a silent mantra, creates vibrational ripples in the subconscious, breaking through layers of resistance and connecting you with deeper planes of consciousness. By committing to even 10–20 minutes a day, you rewire your brain, calm your nervous system, and strengthen the field of intention around you. Over time, meditation changes your vibrational signature. It clarifies the signal you send to the universe.

---

2. Breathwork: Accessing Higher States Through the Body

The breath is the bridge between the conscious and the unconscious, between matter and spirit. When you alter your breath, you **alter your vibration**. **Pranayama**, the ancient yogic science of breath control, includes techniques such as *Nadi□Shodhana* (alternate nostril breathing) and *Kapalabhati* (breath of fire), each designed to purify the body and increase inner energy. **Holotropic or circular breathwork** unlocks non-ordinary states of awareness and emotional release.

- **Box breathing** (inhale, hold, exhale, hold) stabilizes the nervous system and aligns the body with present awareness. When breath is controlled and conscious, your emotions settle. When breath is shallow and erratic, so is your energy. To vibrate higher, you must breathe with intention.

---

3. Food and Water: Fueling the Light Body

What you consume directly affects your consciousness. **Food is information. Water is memory.** Both are vehicles for either coherence or confusion. **Processed, chemical-laden foods** carry low vibrational signatures. They generate inflammation, mental fog, and energetic stagnation. **Living foods**, fruits, vegetables, sprouted grains, herbs, contain biophotons (light energy) and align with your evolving energetic needs. **Water**, when charged with gratitude or structured through prayer or vortexing, becomes crystalline, enhancing cellular communication.

Food prepared in anger, consumed mindlessly, or sourced unethically carries the imprint of those frequencies. As you awaken, your body will crave purity, not just for health, but for vibrational clarity. **Eat in reverence. Drink in gratitude. Your body is a temple. Feed it light.**

---

4. Sound and Frequency: Tuning the Subtle Body

Everything in the universe vibrates. Sound is one of the most powerful tools for retuning the human energy system. **Binaural beats** use two slightly different frequencies to entrain the brain into desired states: alpha for calm focus, theta for creativity, delta for deep healing. **Solfeggio frequencies** (396□Hz, 528□Hz, 963□Hz, etc.) are ancient sound patterns that resonate with the body's energetic centers. **Chanting mantras** like **OM** or **AUM** creates harmonic resonance in the body, awakening dormant awareness.

Listening to music encoded with love, peace, and intention can shift you faster than hours of talk therapy. Conversely, music filled with violence, despair, or objectification keeps your vibration low. **Choose your soundtrack wisely. You are always tuning yourself.**

---

5. Emotional Alchemy: Mastering the Inner Landscape

Emotions are not obstacles to awakening. They are **gateways**. To raise your vibration, you must not bypass your emotional body, you must learn to work with it. **Self-Autolysis** (the practice of questioning beliefs to their core, as taught by Jed□McKenna) helps deconstruct inherited stories and ego attachments. It is ruthless truth-seeking and liberates emotional weight. **EFT (Emotional Freedom Technique)** or tapping releases trauma by combining somatic stimulation with spoken affirmations. It clears energy blockages caused by unresolved emotion.

- **Shadow work, journaling, and inner-child integration** allow you to metabolize grief, fear, and shame, turning emotional lead into spiritual gold. As David□Hawkins taught in *Power vs. Force*, emotions have measurable vibrational frequencies. Shame and guilt rank low, while love and joy resonate high. **Emotional alchemy is not repression, it is transformation.**

---

6. The Power of Intention and Imagination

Intention is the **engine of manifestation**, but intention alone is inert without clarity, emotion, and belief. **Clarity** gives your subconscious a blueprint. **Emotion** energizes the signal. **Belief** determines how well it takes root. Use visualization to feel the life you are calling in. Imagine the version of you who already lives that life. How do they speak? Move? Think? **Now become that version.** Writing your intentions, reading them aloud daily, and visualizing their fulfillment not only activates the Reticular Activating System in your brain (which begins filtering reality accordingly), it also vibrationally attunes your field to the desired timeline.

---

7. The Practice of "Acting As If"

One of the most misunderstood techniques of manifestation is "fake it until you make it." When practiced consciously, it becomes **"embody it until it arrives."** You are not pretending, you are *pre-aligning*. Dress, speak, act, and make decisions from the energy of the reality you desire. Don't wait to feel abundant, **feel abundant and abundance comes**. Every choice is a declaration of identity. **Choose from your future, not your past.**

---

8. Journaling and Conscious Language

Your words are **spells**. Your journal is your **altar**. **Gratitude Journaling** raises your emotional frequency instantly. It tells the quantum field, "I already have." **Intention Journaling** anchors your desires. Be specific, write in the present tense, and embody the version of yourself who already lives it. **Reflective Writing** helps uncover subconscious programs. When you write about your reactions, you begin to see their roots and unhook their power.

Track your dreams. Record synchronicities. Write letters to your future self. **Language creates reality, use it deliberately.**

---

9. Movement: The Body as Portal

The body stores emotion; it also channels divine intelligence. Movement releases stagnant energy and awakens dormant circuits. **Yoga** aligns physical posture with breath and spirit, balancing the *Nadis* (energy channels) and opening the chakras. **Qi□Gong and Tai□Chi** are moving meditations that harmonize life force with breath, increasing internal awareness. **Ecstatic Dance** is a form of surrender that allows suppressed energy to rise and move without mental interference.

The more freely energy flows through the body, the higher your vibrational capacity becomes.

---

10. Nature: The Original Frequency

You are not separate from nature, you **are** nature. Nature is always vibrating in coherence. **Grounding or Earthing** discharges excess static energy and reconnects your body to the Earth's electromagnetic field. **Sun-gazing** (practiced safely at sunrise or sunset) stimulates the pineal gland and synchronizes circadian rhythms. **Forest bathing**, walking barefoot, gardening, or simply watching the wind move through leaves realigns you with the original template of peace.

The further you stray from nature, the more fragmented you feel. **Return to the rhythm. It is your home frequency.**

---

11. Energetic Hygiene and Space Clearing

Your energy field is porous; it absorbs from people, places, and objects. To maintain a high vibration, you must cleanse it regularly. **Smudging** with sage, palo santo, or cedar clears stagnant energy. **Salt baths** discharge toxic frequencies. **Energy healing** (Reiki, pranic healing) restores flow where there is stagnation. Also clear your physical space: remove clutter, bring in plants, play uplifting music, and let natural light enter. **Your outer space reflects your inner state, create a temple, not a prison.**

---

12. Conscious Community and Resonant Relationships

Environment shapes energy. If you spend time with people who dwell in fear, victimhood, or gossip, your field becomes foggy. Surround yourself with: People who speak from love, not lack. Friends who celebrate your expansion, not fear it. Mentors who mirror your next level, not your past self. **You rise fastest in sacred company.**

---

13. The Power of Presence and Surrender

Finally, all techniques must bow to the present moment. You cannot elevate your frequency while grasping at the future or grieving the past. Practice **Wu□Wei**, effortless action. Learn to flow with life rather than push against it. **Surrender doesn't mean passivity; it means receptivity.** The universe responds to alignment, not effort.

---

14. The Throne Method: Sitting in the Already-Realized State

"To sit without asking is to speak the language of inevitability."

Essence of the Method

Known in esoteric circles as 座す者 **(zasu-mono)**, Japanese for *the One Who Sits*, the Throne Method is radical stillness married to absolute conviction. You do not petition the universe; you **occupy** the throne of the Self that already has what you once desired. In Neville□Goddard's language, it is living *in the wish fulfilled.* In Zen practice, it echoes *shikan-taza,* just sitting, yet with a deliberate imaginal seed.

Why It Works

1. **Identity-First Logic**: The subconscious organizes perception around self-image. When you sit as the fulfilled version of yourself, neural predictive coding recruits behaviour to match that identity. **Energetic Coherence**: Dropping verbal affirmations after a single imaginal flash silences inner contradiction. Heart-rate variability rises, and the biofield stabilizes at a frequency reality mirrors. **Quantum Expectation**: Observation collapses probability into form. By refusing to oscillate between the imagined fulfilled state and doubt about its arrival, you hold the quantum field to a single coherent signal, and it responds accordingly.

Closing Reflection

- Your vibration is your cosmic signature, your invitation to the universe. Raising frequency is not escape; it is fuller embodiment. Every breath, bite, word, intention, it all counts. Manifestation is **coherence**, not performance. You do not attract what you want; you attract what you **are**. The Throne Method reminds you that you are already the monarch of your reality. Sit once, rise aligned, and let the kingdom arrange itself accordingly.

You do not need to chase your new reality. You only need to occupy the throne of the Self who already lives it.

Chapter 30: The Only Choice That Changes the Dream

"Love is beyond reason. Logic is beyond feeling. Purpose is the illusion that reconciles the two."

The techniques and practices gathered in the previous chapter are instruments of alignment; they prepare the ground. But beneath all technique, there is a question that no method can answer for you: what will you choose when the noise quiets and only you remain? That question is what this final chapter addresses.

When the war of polarity ends within the mind, there is a quiet that feels almost sacred. The tension that once animated perception begins to dissolve. No longer does the world appear divided into forces that must be conquered or defended against. Light is no longer clung to as salvation, nor is darkness resisted as threat. Success and failure soften. Victory and defeat lose their sharpness. The internal battlefield grows still.

Yet even in this stillness, life does not stop. The body continues breathing. Time continues moving. Circumstances continue unfolding. The simulation does not collapse simply because the mind has reached equanimity. The mirror of polarity may no longer distort perception, but the river of experience continues to flow. And in that flow, action is still required. When you are no longer reacting to opposites, when you are no longer defined by preference or aversion, what then determines your movement? If fear is no longer steering you and desire no longer pulling you forward, what becomes your compass?

The answer reveals itself in a single word: purpose. To be human is to seek meaning. Consciousness does not remain stable in the absence of direction. Without purpose, the mind drifts into fragmentation. Meaning organizes attention. Direction stabilizes identity. Purpose transforms existence from randomness into narrative. It is the invisible thread that weaves isolated events into a coherent story. From an evolutionary perspective, purpose is not merely psychological, it is adaptive. A tribe united by shared meaning survives longer than one scattered by confusion. A civilization guided by common direction builds infrastructure, culture, and continuity. Purpose becomes the architecture of collective survival.

In this sense, purpose can be programmed. It is transmitted through culture, reinforced through institutions, inherited through family structures, encoded in religion, embedded in economic systems, and celebrated through national identity. From childhood, humans are taught what matters. They are shown what success looks like. They are told what is valuable, what is shameful, what is worthy of pursuit. Purpose becomes an operating system. And most programmed purpose serves preservation.

- build wealth, secure stability, protect reputation, preserve identity, compete for advantage, and advance position. This kind of purpose stabilizes civilization. It optimizes survival. It reinforces continuity. It strengthens the architecture of the dream. And because it is rooted in self-preservation, it is predictable. When human behavior is driven primarily by safety, status, belonging, fear, and desire, it becomes highly modelable. Given enough data about motivations, outcomes can be forecast. Logical reasoning, built on risk calculation and reward optimization, narrows the range of possible results. A system does not need to dictate every action if it understands the incentives guiding the actor.

This is the architecture reflected in **The Matrix**. The system relies not on brute force control, but on the predictability of human logic. When individuals act according to optimization, maximizing gain, minimizing loss, the boundaries of outcome remain contained. The illusion of freedom persists, yet the deeper structure remains unchanged. This is what most people call free will. The ability to choose between alternatives. Yet the presence of alternatives does not guarantee freedom. If all options arise from the same conditioning, if each path serves the preservation of self in slightly different ways, then choice becomes variation within constraint. You may choose prestige over peace or comfort over risk, but if the underlying motive remains self-preservation, the deeper trajectory remains similar. The details change. The architecture does not.

The dream continues efficiently. And yet, not all humans behave predictably. Some defy optimization. Some risk advantage for integrity. Some sacrifice security for truth. Some choose compassion when revenge would be justified. Some surrender power when domination would be rewarded. From the perspective of a stability-driven system, such individuals appear irrational. They disrupt equilibrium. They introduce unpredictability. They do not act in accordance with expected incentives.

But unpredictability is not necessarily dysfunction. In biological systems, mutation drives evolution. Without variation, a species stagnates. In ecosystems, disruption often precedes renewal. In personal growth, crisis frequently becomes the doorway to transformation. Predictability preserves what exists. Unpredictability allows what does not yet exist to emerge. Thus, there are two layers of purpose operating within humanity. One sustains civilization. The other evolves consciousness. The first layer ensures continuity. It builds systems, preserves structures, and stabilizes societies. The second layer challenges the limits of those structures. It introduces behaviors that cannot be fully reduced to calculation.

Instinct must be understood carefully here, for instinct is not monolithic. There is reactive instinct and expansive instinct. Reactive instinct arises from fear, insecurity, aggression, unresolved trauma. It destabilizes destructively. It fractures without coherence. It amplifies chaos. Expansive instinct arises from compassion, courage, unity, and love. It does not seek gain. It does not optimize for preservation. It transcends self-interest. It is not chaotic; it is aligned.

This expansive instinct is where transformation begins. A system built upon self-preservation can model self-interest. It can anticipate fear. It can predict desire. It can even contain structured rebellion. It can install guardrails, normalize dissent, and absorb manageable disruption. But when an individual willingly sacrifices advantage for integrity, when love overrides survival calculus, when compassion becomes more important than self-protection, the predictive model falters. There is nothing to threaten.

Nothing to bribe. Nothing to negotiate. The mechanisms of control depend upon leverage. Leverage depends upon desire or fear. When neither governs the actor, the system loses influence. Self-preserving choices are deterministic in the sense that they follow evolutionary programming. They reinforce identity. They maintain structure. They protect continuity. They sustain the architecture of the dream. Selfless choices are emergent. They are non-linear. They introduce variables that cannot be fully anticipated. They operate outside optimization.

This is the anomaly. Not as destruction, but as transcendence of the governing assumption that survival is ultimate. When the self is no longer central, the architecture bends. The system may attempt to contain such anomalies. It may attempt to reframe sacrifice as branding, to commodify compassion, to normalize integrity into marketable identity. It may absorb language while neutralizing impact. But unconditional selflessness cannot be fully reduced because it does not seek dominance within the system. It acts beyond it.

Humanity's reliance on logic is an attempt to create permanence in a world defined by impermanence. We accumulate resources, relationships, knowledge, influence. We build identities anchored in form. We defend narratives. We strategize for stability. Yet impermanence persists. Everything changes. Everything dissolves. Satisfaction built on possession fades. Identity anchored in form fractures. Security rooted in control erodes. Emotion teaches what logic resists. Through love and loss, through joy and grief, through attachment and release, humans learn the central truth of incarnation: nothing can be held forever. The attempt to secure permanence within impermanence creates suffering because form itself is fluid.

Selflessness represents the highest emotional integration of this truth. When you sacrifice for the greater good, you acknowledge impermanence. You loosen identity. You release control. You choose coherence over possession. Integrity is born in this space. Integrity is not rigid morality. It is alignment between inner knowing and outward action, even when action costs comfort or advantage. It is coherence without calculation. It is unity expressed through decision.

Such choices cannot be fully quantified. They are not programmable in the way survival-based decisions are programmable. They arise from awareness beyond conditioning. Free will, therefore, is not simply the presence of options. It is the depth from which action emerges. If action arises from fear, it is reactive. If it arises from logic alone, it is calculable. If it arises from self-preservation, it is evolutionary.

If it arises from unity-consciousness, it becomes transformative. Predictable humans sustain civilization. Selfless humans evolve it. Both are necessary within the dream. But only one alters its architecture. When polarity dissolves, the war within ends. When self-preservation loosens, transformation begins. Free will is not proven by choosing between alternatives. It is revealed when one chooses beyond the self. And that is the only choice that changes the dream.

Continue to the Epilogue: The End of Seeking... **Epilogue: The End of Seeking** There comes a moment, quiet and still, when the seeking falls away. Not because the answers have all been found, or because every mystery has been unraveled. But because something deeper has been remembered, something older than the questions themselves. The flame that once drove the search begins to flicker into stillness, not extinguished by despair, but fulfilled by silence.

This is not the end of the journey. It is the end of the one who journeys. For so long, we've moved through the dream with urgency, grasping for truth, for meaning, for peace. We sought knowledge, power, liberation. We built identities around the seeker, the warrior, the wounded, the wise. But these were costumes worn by the formless. All the while, the stillness within waited patiently, never asking for anything but our surrender.

When we stop seeking and desiring, we come to equanimity. No further movement arises from within. We no longer wish to change the dream, fix the self, or escape the illusion. We no longer try to become, we simply are. And it is this *not trying* that becomes the ultimate surrender. It is not passive. It is not giving up. It is giving *in*, to life as it is, to consciousness as it expresses itself, to the perfection already present in every breath. This surrender is not to another's will, nor to fate. It is to the mystery of being itself. The ego cannot comprehend it. But the Self, which has never been separate, knows it deeply.

In this surrender, you see that all movement, physical, emotional, spiritual, was only ever an echo of forgetting. The striving was sacred, yes. It played its part in the dream. But it is the *ceasing of striving* that unveils the truth. When you stop searching and the need to chase ceases, then this person disappears. The "seeker" dissolves. And what remains is not a perfected version of who you were, but the awareness that was always watching from behind the curtain.

Nothing more needs to be done. The paradox of awakening is that the final step is no step at all. The veil parts not through effort, but through stillness. You see now: the dream was never the enemy. The ego was never broken. The world was never fallen. All of it was a playground for remembrance. And all of it is made of light. You do not need to become anything. You have always been what you are looking for.

And when you are no longer bound by the dichotomies of good and evil, of prison or school, of higher or lower, you begin to see clearly. You are not navigating a construct. You are an expression of the Great Consciousness. A facet of the Supreme Mind dreaming itself through you. And you, in your stillness, are the witness of that dream. The mind may protest. It may return, again and again, with its fears, its needs, its clever riddles. But in the quiet beyond thought, you begin to notice the watcher. The observer. The I Am. That which does not move.

From this space, love is no longer a concept. It is being. Forgiveness is no longer a practice. It is your nature. Suffering is no longer something to resist. It is simply a wave rising and falling in the ocean of peace. The dream continues, but the dreamer is awake. And because you no longer seek contrast, the world no longer needs to echo division. What was once a mirror of imbalance becomes a canvas of peace.

There are no final answers, only final silences. There is no finish line, only the relinquishment of the race. And there is no greater truth than this: what you sought was always with you, because it was always you. You are free now, not because you escaped, but because you remembered. So rest. Breathe. Watch the world move without reaching to control it. Let it all arise and fall, as it has always done. You are not in the dream.

You are the dreamer. And you are home.

Acknowledgments

To awaken is to remember, but the road to remembering is not walked alone. To my beloved wife, Patrycja, thank you for being the reflection of divine love and unconditional support. Your strength and presence have illuminated the darkest parts of my journey, and your belief in this vision helped bring it to life. To my children, Noah, Achilles, and Livia, your innocence, brilliance, and resilience are my greatest teachers. You remind me why we do the inner work: to create a world worthy of your dreams.

To my family and close friends, thank you for walking beside me, for believing in the message, and for being lighthouses in both friendship and faith. Your love is a rare gift, and your loyalty is sacred. To my readers, some of whom are just beginning their awakening, and others who have long walked the path, I thank you. May this book serve not as doctrine, but as a mirror, reflecting the divine truth already within you.

And finally, to my Higher Self, to Source, and to the mystery of consciousness that called this work into being: thank you. For the pain, the joy, the doubt, and the surrender. Every breath has been part of the unfolding.

About the Author

David Ramirez is an author, entrepreneur, and spiritual teacher whose work bridges the worlds of metaphysics, consciousness, and real-world transformation. After a career in military intelligence and private industry, David turned his focus toward uncovering the deeper truths of human existence. He is the founder of multiple businesses and the author of the *Divine Karma* book series, as well as *The Dream of Life*. David's teachings are rooted in lived experience, personal transformation, and a relentless pursuit of truth. He writes not as a guru, but as a fellow traveler, offering insights, stories, and tools for those navigating their own awakening. He currently resides in Miami, Florida with his family and continues to speak, teach, and write about spiritual sovereignty, conscious living, and the hidden architecture of reality.

Epilogue: The Infinite Spiral: Returning Again to Begin Anew

"The dream does not end when you wake. It transforms, and so do you."

For most of human existence, we have treated life as something that happens to us. We have called it fate, circumstance, God's will, karma, luck, or consequence. We have stood inside the experience of living and wondered why certain things arrive and others do not, why some seasons feel like gifts and others feel like punishment. We have searched outward for meaning, for explanation, for someone or something to hold responsible for the shape of our days. But throughout the pages of this book, a different understanding has been quietly taking root, one that changes everything once it is truly received.

The Dream of Life is not a metaphor. It is a description. Life, as you have experienced it (every relationship, every wound, every revelation, every moment of joy and every season of darkness), has been a dream that consciousness is dreaming through you. And now, at the threshold of this epilogue, you are invited to recognize the most liberating truth available to a human being: you did not fall into this dream. You created it.

The Eternal Mirror

Life has always been a mirror. Not a mirror of what you deserve, and not a punishment designed to humble you, but a living reflection of the consciousness you carry within you. Every person who has moved through your life has been a frequency you attracted. Every circumstance you have navigated has been a landscape shaped by your dominant beliefs, your deepest fears, your most persistent longings. The world has not been happening to you. The world has been happening: through you, as you, in response to you.

This is not a cause for shame. The creator does not blame the canvas for what appears on it. The dreamer does not punish the dream for the scenes it generates. To recognize yourself as the author of your experience is not a burden; it is the most profound form of liberation available. Because if you created it, you can change it. If you dreamed it, you can dream differently. If the reflection has been showing you something you no longer wish to see, you have the power to shift the light from which it is cast.

The Dreamer Who Remembers

Awakening is not the act of leaving the dream. It is the act of becoming lucid within it. The moment you recognize that you are the dreamer, everything changes, not the scenery, but your relationship to it. Pain does not disappear. Complexity does not vanish. People do not become simple or transparent. But you begin to move through life with a different quality of presence. You stop reacting as though every event is final. You stop identifying with every emotion as though it were truth. You stop asking the dream to validate you, and begin allowing it to reveal you.

The dream has always been generous in this way. Every heartbreak was showing you where you had placed your worth in something outside yourself. Every betrayal was asking whether you could trust your own perception. Every loss was inviting you to discover what cannot be taken. Every moment of beauty was a whisper from the deep that life, at its core, is not hostile. The dream has been your teacher in disguise, and now that you recognize the teacher, the curriculum begins to shift.

You Are the Author

The most radical implication of everything explored in this book is this: you have been writing the story all along. Not consciously, not always deliberately, not without the invisible influence of generations of conditioning, but at the level where consciousness meets form, you have been the organizing intelligence behind your experience. Every thought that dominated your inner world became a signal. Every belief you held as fixed became a filter. Every emotion you carried unresolved became a magnet. And the dream responded, as it always has, faithfully.

This understanding does not place blame on those who have suffered greatly, for suffering often arises from inherited programs, collective wounds, and conditions far larger than any single individual. But it does illuminate a path forward. Once you see the mechanism, you can work consciously with it. Once you recognize that your inner world is continuously projecting outward into form, you begin to tend your inner world with the same care and reverence you might offer a garden. You begin to weed what no longer serves. You begin to water what you wish to grow.

What Comes After Awakening

There is a question that inevitably arises for the one who has awakened to their role as creator. It is not 'What do I want to manifest?' It is not even 'How do I change the dream?' The question is quieter and more fundamental than both of those. It is simply this: now that I know I am the dreamer, how do I live?

This is where the journey of this trilogy finds its natural next horizon. You have discovered, in the first book, the divine blueprint within you. You have recognized, in the second, that life is a simulation and you are its author. You have learned, in this third volume, how to awaken within the dream and begin creating from wholeness rather than from fear. But wisdom without a way of living is merely philosophy. And so a new question must be asked: what does the awakened life actually look like in practice, breath by breath, moment by moment, in the ordinary and the extraordinary alike?

The Way Forward

The ancient Chinese philosophers answered this question with a single word: Tao. The Way. Not a doctrine to be followed, not a set of rules to be obeyed, but a living relationship with the flow of existence itself. What the Taoists understood, and what the world is slowly remembering, is that the highest form of human wisdom is not the mastery of force, but the mastery of flow. Not the conquest of life, but the art of moving with it. This is what the sages called Wu Wei: effortless action, non-resistance, the profound intelligence of alignment over effort.

In the next book of this series, 'The Way,' we will explore what it means to live as the fully awake observer: present, clear, and no longer governed by the compulsive movements of the reactive mind. We will examine the nature of emotional engagement: how feelings arise not to be suppressed or indulged, but to be witnessed, understood, and gently released. We will explore the paradox of ambivalence, not as indifference, but as the freedom that comes when you can hold any experience without being owned by it. We will look honestly at how the ego recruits emotion as evidence of truth, and how the awakened awareness learns to see through this mechanism without cruelty and without collapse.

Wu Wei is not passivity. It is the most active form of intelligence available to a human being: the intelligence that knows when to move and when to be still, when to speak and when to listen, when to hold and when to release. It is the art of living in harmony with what is, while remaining fully available to what is becoming. It is the recognition that the dream does not need to be forced; it needs to be tended with the same gentle authority with which a skilled gardener tends the earth: neither grasping nor abandoning, but present, attentive, and deeply, quietly alive.

The Dream Continues

You will not finish this book and find yourself suddenly free of all confusion, all doubt, all longing. That is not how awakening works. What you will find, if you have allowed these pages to reach you, is a subtle but undeniable shift in how you relate to the dream. A growing capacity to pause before reacting. A deepening trust in the intelligence of your own experience. A willingness to look at what the mirror is showing you, not with judgment, but with curiosity and compassion. A recognition that the dream is not your enemy. It has never been your enemy.

The dream is your greatest teacher. Your most faithful companion. Your most honest mirror. And now that you see it for what it is, you can stop trying to escape it and begin the far more exquisite work of inhabiting it fully: awake, sovereign, and radiant with the understanding that every moment of this extraordinary, unlikely, unrepeatable life is a scene you yourself have written into being.

The dream of life does not end when you wake. It simply becomes conscious. And a conscious dream, lived from the ground of awareness, is something more beautiful than any philosophy has ever fully described.

The way awaits.

Reflection: The Dreamer Awakens

The Dream of Life is not something that happens to you; it is something you have been creating all along, through every belief you carried, every story you told, every feeling you gave your attention to. Life has been your mirror: faithful, precise, and always reflecting the consciousness you brought to it. To awaken is to recognize this mechanism not as a burden, but as the most extraordinary gift: the knowledge that you are not trapped in the dream, but authoring it. And having remembered that, the next question is not louder or more urgent; it is quieter. It asks simply: knowing all of this, how will you choose to live? The answer, as the next journey will reveal, begins not with more doing, but with a different way of being. The Way is already within you. It always has been.

Appendix: The Gnostic Allegory

For readers wishing to explore the deeper mythological and Gnostic underpinnings of this book's cosmological framework, the following allegory draws on the writings of Valentinus, the Sethian Gnostics, and comparative mythology to illuminate the central paradox of the human condition: are we prisoners, or students? And does that distinction ultimately matter?

"Know what is in front of your face, and what is hidden from you will be disclosed." – Gospel of Thomas 5

Prelude: The Empty Stage

Picture a circular amphitheater whose walls are lined with shifting mirrors. In its center stands a lone actor wearing a blank mask, neither smiling nor frowning, waiting to inhabit whatever role the audience projects upon it. Overhead, a silver sphere rotates, casting light that fractures into a thousand angles. Two doors mark opposite ends of the stage: one labeled PRISON, the other SCHOOL. Tonight's allegory walks through both.

I. Eternity Unfolds: Bythos and the Thirty Aeons

Valentinus, the second-century mystic who almost became Bishop of Rome, taught that before time there was Bythos, depth beyond depth, the Artisan of Silence. From this pleroma, the divine fullness, thirty Aeons emanated in pairs, each one a quality of the infinite: Nous and Aletheia (Mind and Truth), Logos and Zoe (Word and Life), Anthropos and Ekklesia (Humanity and Community). Together they form a cosmic symphony, harmonics of the Absolute playing itself into differentiation.

Modern cosmology, with its talk of quantum fields rippling off a primordial vacuum, unconsciously echoes this ancient intuition: reality is music played on the strings of nothingness. For the Valentinian, the fall from unity was not a moral failure but a structural necessity: differentiation is the precondition for relationship, and relationship is the engine of love.

II. Sophia's Echo: Fall as Pedagogy

Sophia seeks to grasp the source that birthed her. Her desire bends back upon itself, a feedback loop without a partner, generating a vibration too dense for the Pleroma. In classical Sethian Gnosticism this act is a tragic blunder that cracks heaven and ejects a malformed deity, the Demiurge, into the abyss. Valentinus agrees on the rupture but views it through a softer lens: Sophia's misstep is also didactic, planting divine seeds in a lower realm so they may germinate through experience.

Compare this to the Buddhist twelve links of dependent origination: craving leads to becoming, becoming to birth, birth to suffering, but the chain is not condemnation; it is curriculum. Even in physics, high-energy particles collide, creating showers of exotic matter that quickly decay into familiar atoms. The chaos of the collision is prerequisite to the stability that follows.

III. Warden and Schoolmaster: Faces of the Demiurge

The Mask Maker rises from Sophia's discarded light, shaping the raw material of chaos into galaxies, biospheres, and finally human nervous systems wired for storytelling. Sethian texts paint him as an arrogant tyrant who seals the world in heavy matter. Valentinians concede his ignorance but rename it necessity: he is an overzealous pedagogue who drills multiplication tables yet cannot fathom poetry. But what if the Demiurge is more than just a cosmic bureaucrat? What if he is a reflection, a polarized projection, of consciousness itself caught in imbalance: an energetic echo of the mind's investment in control, in separation, in labeling good and evil?

In our era the Demiurge is algorithmic: recommendation engines that reward outrage, news cycles that monetize fear, political theater that converts attention into currency. The same circuitry educates and incarcerates. We may be seeing not an entity, but an archetype generated from the collective psyche of a species still reconciling its polarities.

IV. The Prison Walls and the School Gates

We stand inside a dual-use architecture: brickwork doubles as both bars and archways. When the mind identifies exclusively with the body, the walls tighten into a cell. When awareness recognizes itself as the observer of thoughts, the same walls reveal lessons written in chalk. Prison metaphors dominate apocalyptic media, while school metaphors appear in self-help circles and mindfulness retreats. Neither is wrong; both are lenses on a single phenomenon: consciousness confined within, and refining through, incarnation.

V. Two Maps, One Terrain: Mythic Parallels

To see the universality of this paradox, scan earth's mythic atlas. Across cultures we find the same motif: creation is simultaneously an exile from original unity and an opportunity for growth through engagement with form.

The Sumerian Enuma Elis tells of Tiamat's body split to form heaven and earth, with her defeated monsters becoming servants, a tale of violent ordering akin to the Demiurge's ignorant craft. In the Chinese

Pangu legend, Pangu chisels the cosmos from an egg, holding sky and earth apart for eighteen thousand years before his body becomes mountains and rivers: builder and prisoner of his own project. The Hopi Emergence myth guides humanity through four worlds, assisted by Spider Woman, learning moral lessons in each, a cosmic school with graduation thresholds. In the Maori tradition, Sky Father and Earth Mother cling so tightly their children live in darkness until one son forces them apart, initiating both freedom and responsibility, the bittersweet birth of duality. And in Yoruba Ifa, the Orishas descend to shape the earth yet remain bound by oaths to return knowledge, scientist-teachers of a spiritual academy.

VI. Lessons Behind Bars: Curricular Suffering

Valentinus lists three orders of humanity: hylic (matter-bound), psychic (mind-guided), and pneumatic (spirit-awakened). The Demiurge can instruct the first two but not the third. In practice every person cycles among these states daily: when rage scrolls social media we slip into hylic; when we journal reflections we rise to psychic; when awe silences thought we taste pneumatic.

Three core assignments define the curriculum of incarnation. The first is the discernment of appearances: recognizing propaganda whether from empire, algorithm, or inner critic. The second is the agency of attention: choosing where to shine the inner spotlight, since every thought and choice is a form of investment. The third is compassionate reciprocity: converting survival competition into cooperative inquiry, the uprising that becomes a graduation ceremony.

VII. The Present Scene: A Midterm Exam

Our timeline bristles with tests. AI and deep-fake technology mean the Mask Maker now wields generative tools that can counterfeit any face or voice. Appearances have never been less trustworthy, making discernment both harder and more crucial. Climate extremes collapse infrastructures, revealing the fragility of our shared systems and making cooperation a survival skill. Geopolitical polarization shows that wars of narrative precede wars of artillery. And a rising mental health crisis signals that the syllabus is intensifying, inviting us to ask whether we medicate the inmates or mentor the students. In each headline we can spy two potentialities: reinforcement of confinement, or catalyst for awakening.

VIII. Paths of Liberation and Graduation

Liberation begins with descent before ascent. Just as Sophia must plunge, individuals undertake shadow work: confronting trauma, prejudice, and inherited scripts. Jung called it individuation; Buddhists call it vipassana insight. The Gnostic sacraments, reimagined for the present, look like this: baptism as immersion in sensory presence through cold water, forest bathing, and breathwork; chrism as the anointing of intelligence through study of comparative myth, neuroscience, and ecology; and the Eucharist as communal practice through shared meals, conversation that suspends judgment, and service that asks nothing in return.

Attentional hygiene becomes its own sacrament: designing digital rest periods, curating information intake, practicing single-tasking. These habits starve the prison guards of their preferred currency: scattered attention. Service as skill sharing, offering what you know to those who need it, transforms isolated seeking into collective ascension.

IX. Integration with the Journey

This allegory completes the arc of the book. Chapter 1 unveiled the Dream of Matter; Chapters 2 through 10 charted states of forgetting and emotional alchemy; Chapters 15 through 23 explored quantum and mythic proofs that consciousness sculpts reality; Chapters 24 through 30 offered practical tools for manifestation. This appendix now anchors these insights in a grand cosmology that reconciles two viewpoints: earth as a penal colony of ignorance and earth as a petri dish of enlightenment. The reconciliation is not intellectual but experiential: whichever metaphor you live becomes your reality.

X. Exercises: Prison Break or Final Exam

Mirror gazing: five minutes before bed, stare into your reflected eyes under low light and ask silently, “Who is the watcher?” Note sensations without narrative. Distraction audit: track every digital notification for twenty-four hours and mark each as a helpful lesson, neutral noise, or energy drain; then eliminate one draining item each day for a week. Compassion flip: identify a public figure who triggers you, research a hardship they faced, and journal three sentences acknowledging their humanity. Notice the inner softening that follows. Mythic mash-up: rewrite a personal struggle as a myth blending at least two creation stories from this appendix, then read it aloud and observe any shifts in self-perception. Service lab: offer one skill freely to someone without expectation, and record how giving alters your sense of confinement or community.

Epilogue: Bars That Bloom into Archways

The stage lights dim. The lone actor removes the mask, revealing not a face but a small burning coal. One by one, the spectators feel heat radiate in their own chests. The silver sphere overhead cracks, softly this time, and the shards rearrange into windows that open onto a sunrise. Whether we step out as those who have crossed a threshold or as those who have earned something we cannot fully name is a matter of perspective, not circumstance. The Artisan of Silence smiles from the background of every atom, patient as ever.

May we remember: the same hand that built the wall designed the door. The curriculum ends when the questioner and the questioned realize they are the same light: no longer imprisoned, already home.

www.ingramcontent.com/pod-product-compliance
Lightning Source LLC
LaVergne TN
LVHW010654110826
845149LV00014B/3093

* 9 7 8 0 9 9 8 3 9 3 2 8 5 *